When the myths and stories of a certain place intersect with those of a particular person, a reciprocity of giving and receiving results. After decades of yearning for a return to the beloved west Texas of her youth, Mary Locke Crofts experienced such an encounter when she went to the borderland of Langtry, Texas, to write a dissertation about ancient pictographs. Working from a rented country house near the Rio Grande, Crofts entered in imagination the lives and stories of hunter-gatherers who painted on the canyon walls and in so doing became deeply aware of her own resonances and responses to this mysterious and sacred place. This book bears witness to her journey.

Langtry, Texas

Pathways to Ancient Shelter: A Sojourn in Langtry, Texas

For Heather
with love & appreciation
Mary Locke

3 May 2018

Mary Locke Crofts

authorHOUSE®

AuthorHouse™
1663 Liberty Drive
Bloomington, IN 47403
www.authorhouse.com
Phone: 1 (800) 839-8640

Published by AuthorHouse   02/24/2015

ISBN: 978-1-4969-6933-0 (sc)
ISBN: 978-1-4969-6932-3 (hc)
ISBN: 978-1-4969-6931-6 (e)

Library of Congress Control Number: 2015902006

Print information available on the last page.

Any people depicted in stock imagery provided by Thinkstock are models, and such images are being used for illustrative purposes only. Certain stock imagery © Thinkstock.

This book is printed on acid-free paper.

Because of the dynamic nature of the Internet, any web addresses or links contained in this book may have changed since publication and may no longer be valid. The views expressed in this work are solely those of the author and do not necessarily reflect the views of the publisher, and the publisher hereby disclaims any responsibility for them.

All Fall Down was previously published in the *Cenizo Journal,* Fourth Quarter 2011. *Clinging to the Rock* was previously published in *Poetry at Round Top*, 2014 *Anthology*, Round Top Festival Institute.

Cover image: *View of Langtry*, pulp painting by Beck Whitehead 2006

For
Tom Crofts
Jack Skiles
Wilmuth Skiles
Linda Billings
Pete Billings

The Road Ahead

Whenever we refuse to be knocked off our feet (either violently or gently) by some telling new conception precipitated from the depths of our imagination by the impact of an ageless symbol, we are cheating ourselves of the fruit of an encounter with the wisdom of the millenniums. Failing in the attitude of acceptance, we do not receive; the boon of converse with the gods is denied us.

Heinrich Zimmer, *The King and the Corpse*

When I see the road to Damascus, it is always in my rearview mirror—my epiphanies never strike suddenly. A realization that things have changed, that I have changed, inevitably comes to me gradually.

A new light dawned, however, in Langtry, Texas, where in 2005 I began writing a dissertation about the indigenous rock art. Were I an archeologist, the journey would have been revealed to me differently. But I am a storyteller who was then finishing a study of mythology and depth psychology at Pacifica Graduate Institute in Carpinteria, California.

Storytelling and schoolwork have been consistent passions for me. I relish taking notes and underlining texts. Pacifica's doctoral program, however, goes beyond providing a body of knowledge. Its aims are to shift vision, to enable one to see the world through the lens of myth and archetypal images, and thereby to offer new stories (a kind of *mythopoesis*, myth-making). I didn't buy it at first. Even in my seventh decade, I wanted "real school," not assignments to incorporate my own experiences into papers written in my own voice. I had taught English too long to fathom using first person pronouns in a school paper.

Things happen, though, whether or not one approves or believes. So in the course of life and school and Hindu mythology, I chose as the topic for an early paper the Hindu goddess of creation and destruction, Kali. True to form, she proved to be a powerful energy, a force not to be controlled. As I read and thought and tried to write, Kali chided, mocked, shocked, thwarted, and prodded me to exhaustion. She demanded to be acknowledged yet resisted being organized into paragraphs.

After finally managing to write about Kali, I described my very personal experience with her in a separate essay, "Post Mortem."

Post Mortem

Should anyone ask you to write about Kali, if life is important to you, decline emphatically. When I said aloud, "I'm going to write an eight-page paper on the universal, infinite goddess of death and destruction," a premonition that I was in dangerous territory should have come. It did not.

I know how to write papers. First, you get a topic. Kali does not like to be "a topic." Then you do research. Kali scoffs at the very idea. When you organize a thesis with data and Roman numerals, all hell breaks loose. That hell is Kali herself.

She could not be corralled, much less bridled. She would not be contained. She opposed every sentence I composed. "Contradiction" is far too soft for what she did. She screamed into my ear and would not stop. I am partially to blame for that.

One day in a weak moment, I wrote, "Hello, Kali. I don't know you very well. What do you have to say for yourself?" My naiveté in that moment almost makes me weep. I held my pencil ready for her answer. You can't write the sound I heard as she shrieked, "You! Mary Locke Crosland from the First Baptist Church of Big Spring, Texas! You can't be serious! I wouldn't know where to start with you. They do not even dance in Big Spring!" I meekly replied, "Well, I know something about death." That really set her off. "What do you know about death? I am Hindu, ancient, sacred. I *am* death!"

I am writing this in a tone humorous, which is what I do when I am nervous. What had begun as worry about "the Kali paper" had become fear for my mental stability. Kali was really getting to me.

Finally, one afternoon, I took my computer into the kitchen, stood at the counter and, with hands poised, told Kali she could say whatever she wanted to. She could write this paper herself, free from the confines of graduate school. "I flat give up because I'm going crazy," I told her. In an evil guise of pity, she then allowed me to write as if I had an appointment to interview her at the cremation grounds.

"An interview with the Hindu goddess Kali is an unnerving experience. First of all she won't sit down. She is either hovering over a dead body, or dancing madly, or crouching over Shiva's erect penis." (I first wrote *lingam* but Kali would not have it.) I continued in a light vein describing her horrible hair and nails, but I could not ignore the blood and corpses of babies all around. It thus became clear that Kali is just who she is. No interviewer could ever learn more than that.

That night I had a dream. I was in a tourist court in Mexico, reading *Kalki*, (a book by Gore Vidal I had not looked at in years). In the dream, I kept thinking, "I really shouldn't be reading this book when there is so much to see outside." Then I went to the Embassy where a child killed the security guard. Then my dog escaped from the basement of the motel through the crumbling foundation. I awoke exhausted, went to the computer and wrote my paper. I also went to my therapist and told stories I had never before told about the day my father died.

Kali and Langtry appear to be unconnected in every way. Their paths crossed nonetheless because in Langtry I was thwarted, diverted, frustrated and exhausted by the land and by a writing project that would not fall into place—refused to become what for me would be a "legitimate dissertation." But rather than nudging me into standard dissertation form, Christine Downing (my extremely legitimate advisor) and Carolyn Boyd (archeologist and my external reader) tolerated—even encouraged—my struggle to discover a path that would take me far beyond a school project.

In the end, I had a paper—a doctoral dissertation: *Down into the Abyss, Up into the Shelter: My Journey to the Rock Art/ists of the Lower Pecos Region of Texas.* It consists of a theoretical section, which includes the history of rock art studies and perspectives from which to experience place, a particular place, and a production section of my own experience expressed in poems, essays and a journal. Each chapter of this book is introduced by an excerpt from the theoretical section. The rest is drawn primarily from the production part.

As it was with Kali, I had to surrender, not in defeat but in acceptance. Graduate school or no, legitimate or no, being there and telling this story was not only enough, it was everything.

Orientation

It took so much time to create this place in which time seemed to stand still.

Harry Shafer, *Ancient Texans*

I

Look at the map—
follow the Rio Grande up from
the Gulf of Mexico until you come
to the Devils River and then the
Pecos River twenty miles on west.
That's the country I'm talking about.

It is borderland—
Mexico and Texas meet here,
the Chihuahuan Desert borders
the Edwards Plateau at the southern
edge of the Great Plains.

As you are heading west,
the land changes just before the Devils.
You feel high up in the air, you see farther,
you are in West Texas now.

Highway 90 rises in broad sweeps
and canyons abound.
Most are dry, but watch out
for high water—
especially in the desert.
Out here, we are alert for
anything that moves—
trains, creatures, clouds—
anything at all.

Hawks and vultures watch, too.
As cars go by, they await collisions.
Deer fall by the wayside but
do not remain there long.

In this borderland,
you sense possibilities.
Here the finite seems limitless.

II

Imagine this land covered with water,
say about a hundred million years ago.
When the shallow sea dried up,
dinosaurs left their footprints
and seashells left everything.

Sixty million years ago,
the dinosaurs were gone.
Forty million years ago,
most of the mammals
that followed the dinosaurs,
megafauna,
were also extinct,
and *megaflora* too.

From the top of the next rise,
pull over and imagine the valley a savannah
alive with wonderful creatures.
The vista is large enough,
but water is hard to conjure.
Millions of years, everything shifting
every which way—
rivers form and meanders dig in,
volcanoes lift up and grind down.

Up to ten thousand years ago
during what some call the Pleistocene,
large mammals grazed right here:
mammoths and bison, ground sloths,
glyptodonts and giant armadillos.
New arrivals joined camels, horses, mastodons,
saber-toothed tigers, dire wolves and giant beavers.
The vultures back then were gigantic—they had to be.

III

As animals had migrated here, so did people.
Some say thirty, some say twelve thousand years ago,
the first humans arrived.
Whenever they came and wherever they came from,
they were a hardy lot
moving north and south with the glaciers.
And we know they were right here,
precisely.

Over there by Langtry is Eagle Nest Canyon
where hundreds of bison were chased over the edge
into the waiting arms of butchers
at the ready with their stone knives.
Below the bison bones lie
the bones of a mammoth.
Was it chased too?

IV

Here these hunters and foragers found a land
of water-carved canyons, overhangs for shelters,
and underground caverns and reservoirs.
Limestone is soft and no match
for the power of water and time.
No hurry about it, drop by drop
and eon by eon water etched the desert.

At the end of the Pleistocene,
the weather got hotter and drier
and has been ever since, mostly,
except for a cool spell or blue norther
every now and then.

We have the wood rats to thank
for that weather report.
In little chinks in the rock, they gathered

plants for nests, and miraculously
those nests survived to tell their story:
a bit over two thousand years ago,
the weather took a turn for the wetter and cooler.

V

Like the wood rats' nests
everything here in the lower Pecos,
everything here where nothing
appears remarkable,
everything has a story—
you just have to know how to find it.

Pick up a rock and know ancient oceans.
Pick up some gray dirt and scatter the ashes
of an archaic earth oven.
Pick up a bone and know
someone's dinner on an autumn night
four thousand years ago.

These people were our forebears
on this land and we
their witness-bearers.
We testify each for the other.

1

In the Beginning

In the highlands, you woke up in the morning and thought: Here I am, where I ought to be.

Isak Dinesen, *Out of Africa*

Physical contact, mental contact, spiritual contact—all depend upon how one looks at an encounter, how one names it, what one desires from it, and with what humility one approaches it. With intention, reflection, and surrender, with body, heart, and mind, I seek to cross the threshold to the mythos (stories), ethos (character), and pathos (feeling) of this desert canyon country.

November 11, 2005 Friday

I am listening to music from *Out of Africa*. The view of the Rio Grande bottoms from the top of the cliff reminds me of the view from the rim of the Ngorongoro Crater in Tanzania and moves me deeply.

I arrived in Langtry at dusk two nights ago. The Skiles (Jack and Wilmuth) handed over the key to the little brick house (built to be a country church) and I moved in—books mostly. I tried not to bring them, but I told Tom [my husband] that if I were being who I am and not who I'm supposed to be, I would have books with me. I have a radio but no television and no telephone.

I have arranged my computer on the table so I can look straight out the front door with windows to my right and left. I am looking at Mexico, right there across the river from the old Skiles place [Guy and Vashti Skiles, Jack's parents]—a line of cliffs, black and beige, green hills above, and a desert meadow nearer with brush in many shades of green. My house sits on a narrow road that loops through Langtry off U.S. 90. Out the door I see the Border Patrol driving by. Out my left window, a train rattles down tracks paralleling the highway on the way to California. Big trucks truck along beside them. A mesquite tree filters my view of the deserted tourist court and store where the Border Patrol vehicle (white SUV with green letters) is now parked. I have already seen quite a few of them. At one big checkpoint between here and Del Rio, everyone heading west is stopped for questioning.

The sun is just now breaking through the clouds at 7:30. I have been waiting for it for over an hour but only now is it showing its face.

I tried to imagine Father Sun yesterday when it appeared huge and orange between the hills and the clouds. Father Sun, whose appearance you cannot assume, who is prayed up each morning by elders and welcomed by all creatures, great and small—(all creatures are small, relatively speaking!)

I left the house at 6:40 a.m. with just enough light to see snakes on the road, but when one appeared, I almost did not see it. Again I went toward Guy and Vashti's rock cottage. Looking into the canyon to the right, I heard hog sounds (javelina? feral?) and saw something move in the bushes near me. What I first thought was a big raccoon

3

turned out to be a huge porcupine standing stock-still right in the open. I moved away to my left and it moved away to its right and straight off the cliff. I looked over and saw nooks and crannies in the cliff wall that are hard to see unless something moves inside. The porcupine was beautiful—not spiny but fluffy looking and sweet.

I looked over into the greater canyon with all the shelters—a dry creek bed at bottom and on top a windmill with turkey vultures perched on the vanes. One swooped over to check me out. It was much larger close up than it had looked circling high.

I walked down the steep road into the canyon and around a cliff. Unsure which way to go at a fork and wary of running into a feral hog, I turned back toward home. Those wild hogs are very frightening creatures, aberrations—farm hogs grown huge with long wiry hair.

On the way back home, I almost stepped on a small snake on the road—about twenty inches long, gold-green with a black head. It was as slender in diameter as a dime or a quarter or a nickel, I don't know. It sat so still I thought it might be dead, but when I tickled its tail (do snakes have tails?) with a stick, it "essed" its way across the road and quickly disappeared into the brush. Perfect camouflage.

I am trying to make this about me and here and now—my body, my heart, my soul, my story. I just now remembered that a long time ago Dennis [Dennis Slattery, Pacifica professor] suggested that I go away for a few weeks and write about my experience in the wilderness. Now I am doing that very thing and my brain moves all ways, always.

The first Skiles came here from Kentucky and Karnes City, Texas—a plantation lost after the Civil War. Jack's granddaddy brought his father Guy here in 1903 when he was five. Jack grew up exploring these canyons and caves. Now in his seventies, he keeps up with the land and sheep and the community: water, schools, roads, church. He has written a book about Langtry, *Judge Roy Bean Country,* and has another in the works. His wife Wilmuth is from Mertzon, a little town north of here, and is a retired teacher. They met at Sul Ross State in Alpine.

Last night Jack came over with his son Raymond who for eighteen years has been a biologist at Big Bend National Park. It sounds like the perfect job to me, so I asked how he had managed not to get promoted to a higher desk job. He said he had resisted the Peter

Principle. Jack said he doubted if any of his children would ever come back to live in Langtry.

It is sad to contemplate that the long history of Skiles in Langtry could ever come to an end. But that happened to my family in Palo Pinto County on the Crosland farm on Dotson Prairie and the Costello ranch up at Pickwick on the Brazos. No Croslands and no Costellos remain where my ancestors lived and worked and loved the land, felt kin to it, could not imagine that there would come a day when none of their family would be there.

Yet in the course of things, of course, the truest thing is change and change courses through both endings and beginnings, though beginnings, to me, do not seem as solid as endings. The joy of a good beginning does not hold a candle to the bone-piercing pain of an unwanted ending.

I was talking recently about the archaic people of the lower Pecos and their art with a man who said, "I can't stand the thought that it is going to end." I said, "Do you mean the world as we know it, or the environment, or you yourself?" He said, "I am pretty self-turned." So I assume he was thinking about his life in this place, all the beauty and mystery, and the fact that he must leave it, sooner or later. His wife told me he was going in for a heart test next week. Maybe he was thinking of his heart in a way he had not thought of it before—his very real heart in his very real body that will shockingly, incredibly stop and the rhythm it has maintained all these years end.

Yesterday, when I got up, I said to myself: "Whatever happens today is what is supposed to happen. It is the right thing." I was preparing myself for vicissitudes. Chris [Chris Downing, my Dissertation Advisor] says that I am the only person she knows who uses the word *vicissitudes* all the time. I am surprised that it is not the most common word.

To try to gather myself, I am going to find a good quotation to meditate on. I will start with a passage from Thomas Merton's *Asian Journal*: "Our real journey in life is interior; it is a matter of growth, deepening, and of an ever greater surrender to the creative action of love and grace in our hearts. Never was it more necessary for us to respond to that action."

An interior life? I have never been that good at that. Is that what this is all about? Forcing me inside? Pushing (or pulling!) me inward from the far outside I have always dwelt in?

5

Here in this red brick house in Langtry, I cry as I write. A strange miracle that I am here. I can't really say how it happened. I have always imagined myself writing in a cabin in the West, but I did not connect that imagination with *this* little house in the West. Rather, I strained and struggled to come out here to do a job—onerous, heavy, impossible. Yet Merton says I should "surrender to the creative action of love and grace" in my heart. Creative action is what I need, but from love and grace? in my heart? really?

Surrender—a gesture of not being in charge and, if I am not in charge, who is? what is? Do I have to believe something in order for this creative action of love and grace in my heart to be available—able to avail, prevail, unveil?

It is 8:17 p.m. At dusk I get depressed and discouraged. I wonder if my problem is not eating right. I had left-over chicken and cheese-on-toast and a cookie for supper. Anyway, I don't see how I can do this dissertation at all. I have been sorting my papers this evening. Nothing creative at all—watched part of *Harry Potter*.

Tonight I think I am crazy trying to write a dissertation and/or spending a month out here alone. At sunset, I walked back over to the Skiles' cottage on the canyon edge. The same snake crossed the road at the same place it crossed early this morning—a sign. This is truly wonderful country. I found bones—maybe a bird? I'm not sure.

Tomorrow I go home for a bit. I don't like being away from Tom. Home on weekends? I don't know.

The moon is almost full.

Sweet dreams.

Found Wanting

All journeys have a secret destination of which the traveler is
unaware.

Martin Buber, *The Life of the Hasidim*

My destination is
the land of the Pecos River,
the Devils River and the Rio Grande
where I will reflect upon rock art
painted on canyon faces
four thousand years ago.
My intention is to discover some true thing
and tell that story.

My path to the rock art
twists down the mountain,
across the ridge and
up into shelter with painted walls.

I find myself in completely
unfamiliar territory—
I am anxious and self-conscious,
I want to become on the spot
a wise philosopher, a discerning scientist,
a keen perceiver, an incisive translator.
In fact, I am naïve, romantic,
enthusiastic about all the wrong things.

I strongly desire something from this place
and these ancient figures.
What brought these strange
figures to this hidden wall
and me here as witness?
I strain to open not just my eyes
but my whole self.
And I do not even know what that means.

Seeing Games

Dancing myself
into a trance is
not my culture.
Though tempted,
I am terrified of
that much surrender.
I would like to be a seer
but scarcely see what is
right in front of me.

I play vision mnemonics:
look at that snake, notice texture,
attend to light and shadow,
focus on form, line,
color, tone, context,
and movement, especially movement.

Still I miss so much.
"If it had been a snake,
it would have bitten me."
Once it was a snake, a king snake,
and I did not see until I almost
stepped on it, even though
I was looking for snakes.

See and name: wickiup circle, tipi rings,
Rio Grande vega covered with cane.
See and name: ancient images drawn
in the shelter in the canyon.

See and name: a start but
not enough. I want more
even though I fear what might
be revealed and I dread
what might be asked of me.

Clinging to the Rock

The sky overwhelms me.
I squat low on the edge of the canyon
even when no vultures
swoop above me.

The Rio Grande moves on around
the bend. I do not flow with it.
Sirens call, but I do not follow.
I cling to the rock.

If I were to let go to this place,
to these people, to my longing,
were I to let go, I might disappear
forever.

For now, I yield only to
this one piece of quartz
sparkling in the slant
of the morning sun.

2

My Name is Called

Here is the time for the *sayable, here* is its homeland.
Speak and bear witness. More than ever
the things that we might experience are vanishing, for
what crowds them out and replaces them is an imageless act.

Rainer Maria Rilke, *Duino Elegies*, "The Ninth Elegy"

Naming is a part of my process of learning to see and to hold in memory. Repeatedly I name silently, aloud, and in the written word: sky, clouds, stars, moon, Milky Way, sunrise, sunset, rock, shrub, fossil, snake, spider, bees. This is my life in Langtry: birds, bugs, porcupine, deer, wild hogs, Border Patrol. Rilke says naming may be our highest calling, but naming is much more than saying a word—it is seeing, acknowledging, evoking, remembering, communing.

November 13, 2005 Sunday

Sunday morning in my little church house. (I imagine hymns sung right here—though it was Church of Christ—no piano!) I am listening to a CD of the world's sacred music, Native American now: "Yo way o way, yo way o hi ya, yo wayo heya, hey yo, hey ya, yo, yo a way."

I left for my walk at 6:45 a.m. Decided to go back to Guy and Vashti's, wondering what surprises awaited. I went to the head of the first canyon and found neck and other bones from I know not what—bones scattered all about. Then I smelled something dead and found a rotting carcass nearby, a ringtail cat? Its skin is still partly attached and it is screaming. I shudder to remember it, dead and screaming.

Then to the big canyon overlook. A small feral pig was moseying along the little road at the bottom, all alone, no worries, seemed to know where it was going.

I tried to imagine the people of the shelters awakening and greeting the sun as I did with "Ya, ya, heya," and then I sang over the cliff, "Morning has broken, like the first morning." The sun was higher in the sky than I expected when it cleared the clouds. I made up words to "Morning Has Broken": "I find myself here, I don't know why. What am I to do, where am I to be? Don't know where I'm going, or what I'm going to do when I get there."

As I write, beautiful big birds appear out the window—yellow chests, stripes on head, multi-colored wings, pink legs. Two walk along together pecking, pecking. A third follows behind. I think I found them in the book, meadowlarks. I'm not that good at bird identification—except vultures and sparrows.

I followed the fence on the edge of the canyon back to the cottage. Another vision of Ngorongoro—I would be looking for elephants and giraffes and lions and zebra were I in Africa. Here I look for deer and smaller critters, lizards, spiders—anything moving.

The little rock house reminds me of my own family's farmhouse up in north Texas. I walked around the swimming tank in the back, found beautiful colored glass scattered all about. (I brought some pieces home: purple, blue, violet, aqua, and multicolored. I have them propped up on the screen door.)

Then I saw something that made me laugh out loud. On the window of the shed behind the house is a sign with only one word: *CROFT*. No *s* but *my name*! The gods are so funny. I thought, I don't believe in miracles, but I have them anyway. It looks like this place has called my name.

I wish I could do better on my project. Would I be here now if I had no project? very, very likely NOT. I look at the cliffs and the hills and more hills beyond. It is hazy in Mexico and cloudy-hazy here.

So: Merton: "creative action of love and grace"? "interior"? Does this particular exterior help me become more interior?

I am all the time reminded of when I was a kid in Big Spring, Texas, wandering around alone—just ambling along, looking, listening, talking to myself.

In light of that, I'll try another reflection, this time with a passage from James Hillman's *Healing Fiction*: "The way we imagine our lives is the way we are going to go on living our lives. God and myth are in the rhetoric—the way we use words. For the manner in which we tell ourselves about what is going on is the genre through which events become experiences."

I have known that what I told myself about coming out here, leaving Tom, spending money, being adventuresome—the way I framed this trip—would determine how I lived it and felt about it. That is what Hillman is saying. I'm just not sure how much my story determines my actions, but I know it shapes my meaning. Stories seem to have a life of their own. In other words, am I that much in charge?

What genre am I living in? a fairy tale, a poem, a comedy, a tragedy, a *bildungsroman*, a quest? Yes, quest. The truest thing about me is that I am a seeker, but what do I seek? If this really is not about the dissertation but, in fact, about me, then who am I in this story? What part do I play?

I was thinking this morning about my goddess spirit. I thought I was Artemis, but she has more intensity than I. Then I thought of Athena, but she takes herself too seriously. I thought about Aphrodite—the closest to me I think.

So, Aphrodite, are you giving me tasks—sorting, discerning the right time, climbing high, going into the depths, yielding to temptation? Are there helpers for me?

Back to Hillman:

> Rhetoric means the art of persuasion, and
> the rhetoric of the archetype is the way each God
> persuades us to believe in the myth that is the plot
> in our case history. But the myth and the God are
> not something set apart, to be revealed in numinous
> moments of revelation, by oracle, or through
> epiphanies of images. They are in the rhetoric itself,
> in the way we use words to persuade ourselves about
> ourselves, how we tell what happened next and answer
> the question *why*.

I think he is speaking mostly about stories we tell in therapy, but their power prevails no matter where we tell them. Certainly they change through time—new perspectives, different language.

It is almost 10 a.m.—my scheduled time of departure for San Antonio and my other home. I could wait until 11. Compromise! Leave here at 10:30, so I get to play for thirty more minutes. A bird clinging to my screen door says: "Yes, stay—that is the right thing to do." Small, pale gray stomach, some kind of sparrow. It is rearing back to look in the window.

Mary Leslie [Leslie Middleton, a Pacifica classmate] said my project is to take myself seriously. Could it also be to "answer the question *why*" or even to believe (!) there is a why even if we do not know what it is? An outer why? An inner why?

Hearts Desire

[I seek] to understand various ways in which men of different traditions have conceived the meaning and the method of the "way" which leads to the highest levels of religious or of metaphysical awareness.

Thomas Merton, *Mystics and Zen Masters*

I seek what Merton sought—
to know how people have conceived
and communicated with
the spirit—"God," some call it,
sometimes forgetting that that word
is the biggest metaphor of all.

I joke that knowing the gods to be
ineffable never made anyone
stop talking about them—
quite the opposite, in fact.

But it is no joke that we seek
ways to speak *to* the gods.
Whether they are listening
or whether they are not,
we must speak our longings
even so.

And Then One Day

Approaching ancient rock art,
I search for a story, any story to
bring order to the chaos on the wall and
in my mind:
Long ago in canyons of the lower Pecos—

At its beginning, a story lies
between teller and listeners,
but soon it encompasses both, soon
all wander together in
Lower Pecos canyons.
But a setting is not story.
It needs characters to stir it up.

Long ago but not so far away—
right here, in fact—
nomadic people hunted small animals,
gathered roots and cacti for sustenance,
and painted myriad figures, some human
with animal parts, some all monster,
some geometric, some organic.
Many of their paintings remain.

Nomadic travel, hunting, gathering, painting—
my characters are on the move,
but the real story begins
when the storyteller says:
And then one day, something happened,
something unusual.

My problem now is that
no one knows exactly who these
people were, where they came from,
where they went, the moments
of their days. We have few
clues to their ideologies,
cosmologies, theologies.

Many archaeologists steer clear
of rock art or else cling
to the first of the story—
describing, setting the stage.
Scientists need proof.

But I am not an archaeologist.
I am a storyteller
with an imperative for truth
but not necessarily for facts.
Facts can be listed,
stories must be woven.

I cannot know the stories
of these people,
not in fact. Yet, in reverie,
I walk with them
down canyon paths.
I sit with them in shelters,
listen to them speak
and weave my story—
their story.

3

Straightening My House

The interior landscape responds to the character and subtlety of an exterior landscape; the shape of the individual mind is affected by land as it is by genes.

Barry Lopez, *Crossing Open Ground*

Though I do not know how the people of the lower Pecos understood their myths, I have no doubt that they had them and that they are reflected in some mysterious (to me, and, also, perhaps to them) manner in the rock art images. I do know that the people who now live in the lower Pecos country have myths and sacred stories that grow out of their lives in this place.

November 17, 2005 Thursday

I got back from San Antonio a bit before noon after stopping at the coffee shop in Uvalde for breakfast and at the Mexican grocery store in Del Rio. I brought lots of books back but not too many, never too many.

I sat behind the house (it is cold and windy) and walked around looking for stuff—rocks, glass, bones—and wrote "Lee Side." Now I'm going to drive to the top of the hill to make a couple of calls. It is too windy to walk. How could those hunter-gatherers live in cold and windy weather? by huddling around a fire at the back of the shelter? piling on skins and mats? piling on each other?

I have been crying a lot this afternoon and feel tired though it is only 4 p.m. I played Jessye Norman and I cried at "Amazing Grace" and everything else. I feel lonesome and feel like lonesome is all the some there is. When you aren't lonesome, you are kidding yourself—working real hard not to notice.

It is 5:47 p.m. and the sun is going down and the wind is rattling my windows. I want to be sure to see the moon come up (one day past full). I rearranged my rooms, drank hot chocolate, talked to Tom. Finally took a walk—saw no animals, but I found that *CROFT* is on the front of that shed as well as on the back.

When I told my friends at book group and at dream group about this adventure, they thought it was great—significant, brave, a soul journey, but I don't know how to do a soul journey. One good piece of advice: get my house straight and leave it alone. That's not that hard for me, the leaving it alone part.

I have heard it said that people sometimes go crazy when they are all alone.

Lee Side

The rolling plains with fields of grain, wheat billowing in the wind, are often imagined as an ocean.

West Texas causes no one to imagine an ocean, the only billowing is of bed sheets on the line, but here it takes absolutely no imagination to know the wind.

In Big Spring, I spent most of recess at Airport Elementary trying to press my skinny body against the lee side of the building, in the sun, out of the wind and out of view of my teacher. All I remember of playing Red Rover is the sting of sand on my legs.

Today in a more southerly part of West Texas, two hundred miles straight south to be exact, I am sitting in the sun on the lee side of the little church, now the house that is my retreat. Warm when the sun shines through the clouds but quickly chilled when it does not, I face west, seeking inspiration.

I am looking at small sage bushes, prickly pears, a juniper bush, a mesquite tree, and grass that does not billow but holds its bow. There is no letup in the wind to allow waves.

I have returned to Langtry, a little town right on the Rio Grande, bringing my body and spirit if no clear thought. I think the house missed me and was glad to hear my key turn in the lock, the door swish across the carpet, and the screen door slam hard in the wind.

It is Thursday. Last Thursday I came with a few clothes, a little food, and many books. I brought candles and my mountain lion fetish to begin my altar. I have added rocks, a feather, a dead scorpion, and the skeleton of a pygmy lizard.

I was here for three days and then I went back home. Leaving home is hard; leaving here is hard.

I don't feel just right either place. I trust that I will come to know why I am here.

The official purpose is to write my dissertation on the rock art on the wind-carved canyon shelters of three rivers, the Pecos, the Devils, and the Rio Grande. I walked over to the canyon edge just now, even in this big wind. I love to look at the dry creek bed between the sheer walls of Eagle Nest Canyon.

Ever alert for creatures, today I saw only tracks. Then I noticed the huge fossils on the rock beneath my feet and I discovered an ocean after all—the ocean that once was here—unimaginable, but a fact—a hundred-million-year-old fact.

Back at the house, I decide to see exactly what "lee side" means. Definition number one: "*naut.* the side away from the wind." Definition number two: "Cover, shelter." It may not seem like much to some people, but it jolts me. I am many decades away from the leeward wall of my school, where I sought protection from stinging dust storms. I am miles away from any ocean. I am, however, seeking shelter.

Sometimes even the lee side does not always provide respite. For example, just after "lee" here in my *American Heritage Dictionary* is the entry "Lee, Ann" and it happens that this afternoon in a little town in Georgia my sister-in-law is attending the funeral of her niece Lee Ann. Alone and lonely, in the desert wind, I feel the great sorrow of the death of a child, only thirty years old. Where is the lee side here? Where respite, where comfort, where shelter from the sting?

Canyons Surprise

On the road to Langtry, Texas,
and Eagle Nest Canyon
with its shelters of painted walls,
I study things—
fences, gates, telephone poles,
dusty roads fading over the hills,
railroad tracks, a train now and then,
a falling down corral by a falling down house,
the husk of an old tourist court,
vultures, hawks, deer,
some dead, some not.

Occasionally I see cross-country bikers,
some pull small trailers.
One had a dog sitting under his awning
like an Indian pasha.
What could that dog have been thinking?

Turning onto Texas Loop 25
toward the Rio Grande,
I enter the land of canyons.

It is hard to get hold of a canyon—
it attracts and repels simultaneously.
Some are deep, many hidden.
Many a time, walking along a mesa top,
I look down and am shocked to find myself
on the very edge of an abyss.

I had been in Langtry a long time
before I saw Crack Canyon
right downtown.
"Go to the community center," I was told,
"past the barbeque pit,
on beyond the swings."

The canyon is deep and wide.
How could I have missed it?
Actually I had seen its beginning,
a small arroyo by the road, a dip really.
I had no imagination that very quickly
the bottom fell out.

There is a lot to say about canyons,
but the first thing to know
is that they are dangerous.
From the edge, you look straight down,
far down.
If you should fall, slip off,
be blown by the wind,
you die.
Simple as that.

One teenager did—
died.
There was drinking involved, they say.
He was laughing with friends,
pissing off the edge of Pump Canyon
and then he was gone—
the wind might have helped,
and the alcohol.
Had to get the boat to go up the
river to get him.

His friends said they were sure he stood
up after his fall.
Those who found him said "No way, not
with that many broken bones."
I believe them both. Out here,
contradictions are the norm.

Other things can help you over the edge,
rattlesnakes, for example.
At Victoria Falls in Zimbabwe, I was told
that tourists die every year—
caught between the chasm and a pit viper,
they take the chasm.

I always think of that story
here in the canyons of Langtry.
I stay my body's length
from the precipice, aware that even
a sudden flush of wild turkeys
might surprise me to death.

4

Awareness of the Source

The loss of imagination is also the loss of soul. When you can't feel the tug in your psyche toward a stone, something essential is lost: a connection, a sense of meaning, an imaginative spark. The touch of myth.

D. Stephenson Bond, *Living Myth*

Understanding traditional uses of stories enhances my imagination of the myths and legends given breath around the ancient shelter fires. The ashes of those very fires remain piled ten to twenty feet high in some of the larger shelters and connect me to eons of fires and to past generations of stories that were nurtured in their warmth.

November 18, 2005 Friday

I went to bed about 9 p.m. I tried listening to Spurs basketball but even with my short-wave radio, reception was lousy so I fell asleep and dreamed a lot—something about this house coming apart.

I woke up early and decided to bundle up and go for a walk. For the first time, I went to what was once the center of town and to the canyon beyond. Looking back up the hill, I realized that particular canyon is visible from my front steps, but I had never seen it—or realized that what I was seeing was it!

Today is very cloudy and windy and coldish (only fifty but it feels colder to me). Moody weather appropriate for the Native American flute music I am listening to. Lonesome deep tones—held long, barely moving—that sound like the wind blowing over the tops of the old bottles I found yesterday.

There are more falling apart houses here than livable ones. Long after the roofs have caved in, large rectangular stones and small filler stones fall one by one—dilapidating the once proud structures. I can tell by faded signs that some were businesses—grocer, barber, ice house. Others were homes. I try to visualize what Langtry was like when it was a thriving place.

The Torres house belonged to one of the first families of Langtry. They also built a sort of stone labyrinth over by the Eagle Nest Canyon. It is about four feet high, probably a pen for sheep—I have not explored it because it looks like rattlesnake heaven. Near there are the remains of a wonderful stone wall across the slope that is the entrance into the canyon. The Torres men lugged all those huge stones in there to keep the sheep from wandering to the edge and slipping over.

No Torreses here now. Buzzards are the only living thing to be seen around their old place. Time and death. Change and loss. Everywhere, of course, but so noticeable here where the land and the people now and for thousands of years have been wind brushed, sky viewed, sun cooked, and moon showered.

Last night the just-past-full moon came up so fast, so large, so golden. I was thrilled to see its ragged edges clearly without the binoculars and imagined that the earliest people felt the same awe and amazement each time the moon rose—now larger, now smaller,

31

and then not there at all. I know why the lighted part wafts and wanes as they likely did not, but I don't remember it easily. I have to concentrate to remember that it is not actually changing size, that one half is always illuminated.

Moments: when I got here yesterday, I felt so lonesome I cried. The emotion arose from memories of my parents and grew into sadness that life is short and that we can't seem to appreciate it until it is gone (or almost gone). Then I opened Witter Bynner's *Laotzu* to find an old piece of paper that revealed that on September 4, 1941, my father had paid a five dollar fine to the city of West University Place. I don't think it is his writing, but it shows an actual moment of his life—a moment remembered now sixty-four years later—my father's presence there at municipal court. He died forty-four years ago when I was 17. I remember very few of his moments.

Now I am listening to the flute play and writing my morning reflection. I will turn again to Thomas Merton and *New Seeds of Contemplation*:

> Contemplation . . . is a spontaneous awe at the sacredness of life, of being. It is gratitude for life, for awareness and for being. It is a vivid realization of the fact that life and being in us proceed from an invisible, transcendent and infinitely abundant Source. Contemplation is, above all, awareness of the reality of that Source.

I am curious about that Source. It puzzles me.

Then I came across notes on Paul Tillich's *The Courage to Be*. I will go back later to find his actual words. This seems to be my paraphrase:

> All human beings have a sacred dimension.
> We find it in our ultimate concern,
> in movement of desire—[not *getting* our deepest desire but whatever our desire is];
> feelings, values, intentions which motivate what we do and think;
> interior movement of Self in unfolding of our lives.
> This movement of the spirit is driven by images,

32

images become stories.
Inner dynamic of spirit is expressd in story, ritual,
image,
and these expressions shape the spirit.
Sacred story, ritual, image can restrict or release
movement of spirit.

This idea recurs in much of my reading: the shaper being shaped, and the spirit and the images in constant creation of each other. It seems to me that Tillich is right about stories.

I try to project this idea on the lower Pecos hunter-gatherers. I ponder motivating desires, interior movement of the spirit driven by images, stories, ritual. Even though I have no idea what "inner dynamic of spirit" the painters intended to express, the painted images must have been part of sacred rituals and stories. How did these strange (to me) figures restrict or release movement of spirit of these people?

They had to get through the day—eat, hunt, fish, gather, grind, make tools and ovens, prepare the food, cook, commune, communicate, make decisions, deal with dangers and fears. And now I wonder: did they think about meaning? about more than survival, about being part of a longer, larger story? about tribes, ancestors, this world and the Other World?

We do not know, but we have some hints. The paintings are not of trees, people, or daily life but of strange figures and symbols. I believe these images reflect a movement of spirit, deep desire, communion more than communication. Does time mean anything to the human spirit? Obviously, expressions of the spirit do change, but it seems to me there is something essential that never changes.

Each morning for thousands of years people out here have opened their eyes to the very same land I see. I imagine that they awoke with hopes and intentions and that the deepest of these reflect their imagination of the sacred. You can see it in their handwork. They wound, knotted, and wove the smallest string from a lechuguilla leaf into fine thread to make beautiful, delicate pouches and nets. They carved sticks and stones to make elegant tools. Even their rough sandals are elegant. All a testimony to the fact that "primitive" is not simple or crude. All a testimony to their spirit.

Soaring and Descending

Out here, the sky and wind are the world I live in.
In the city, I am not that aware of the sky.
Occasionally I look for
rain clouds or seek Orion or
check the moon's cycles,
but out here, I look up all the time—
I have no choice.
To look at all is to see the sky.
The horizon is always right in front of me.

I also look down at the earth and my feet upon it.
Otherwise, I might step into a creature's hole
or upon the creature itself
or I might stumble over rocks and ledges.
Here in the world of snakes, cactus,
and canyons, not looking down
would put me in mortal danger.

Looking up and looking down are also
ways of orientation in internal landscape.
Direction matters. Paul Tillich used the term
"ground of one's being" to point to ultimate
desires of the human spirit.
James Hillman distinguishes between
soaring upward in spirit toward wholeness
and enlightenment
and plunging downward with soul
into conglomerations, endarkening.

I try to imagine hunter-gatherers
soaring and descending,
enlightened and endarkened.
My desire stirs their spirits.
Their spirits whet my desire.

Around the Bend

Three canyons over from Crack Canyon
is Eagle Nest Canyon.
You can choose your path to the canyon floor.
Here you slip straight down through a cut,
climb over boulders and slide down scree.
Grab a limb and you'll regret it—
everything has thorns.
Over there a bit you might take
the horse trail, or at least that's what it was
for a hundred years or so.

Folks have been climbing around
these canyons for thousands of years.
Grinding holes and smooth stones,
manos and *matates*, tell of
women moving by season,
by sunshine and wind,
seeking a comfortable place to work,
telling stories, and watching
their children galumphing
around the canyon creek.

It's fairly easy to walk on the canyon floor,
but a cautionary note—
that boulder, the one the size of
a small barn, was five hundred yards
up the canyon
until the flood of '56.

Scramble up the scree up into Eagle Nest Shelter
and appreciate its magnitude.
The floor built up over fifteen feet
reveals ages of life here.
The paintings on the north wall
are mysterious, indescribable—
there is no word, not even a metaphor.

Imagine those who painted
on the walls, ground the acorns,
built the fires. Now look out to
study the canyon.
Rumor has it that
bison and mammoth bones lie
just around the bend. We must
move on into the deepening
shadows.

All Fall Down

When I first saw the old store,
the roof had fallen but not
all the way down. The rafters slanted
from the top of the high adobe walls
to the dirt floor—at midmorning
drawing a maze of shadows over
etchings made by spiders,
lizards, and snakes.
Yet the front of the building stood tall,
J. P. TORRES, DRY GOODS &
GROCERY bold above the old door
permanently ajar.

The Torres Store was built in late
eighteen hundreds on Torres Street,
the main street of Langtry, Texas,
which sits on a northern hump of the Rio Grande
upriver the Big Bend,
the Gulf of Mexico far downstream.

Termed "ghost town" in most books,
Langtry is in fact home for
about twenty people—though numbers
matter not at all to its essence.
The Torres Store is one of about
a dozen old buildings —some
inhabited, some uninhabitable,
most somewhere in between,
empty but not gone.

The Torres place was the patriarch—
a Langtry attraction, a place of pilgrimage.
Early on, the Torres men had bargained
with the Galveston, Harrisburg, and
San Antonio Railway to make a
loop through town (mirroring

the Rio Grande's loop north)
in trade for water for their steam engines.
A deal was made and water was
pumped far up from Osman
Canyon, ever after, in these parts,
called "Pump Canyon."

Enterprising folks, the Torres family
ran sheep. Still standing are two
of their pens—one a roofless labyrinthine
rock shelter and, even more impressive,
a massive rock fence built across
a cut into Eagle Nest Canyon. Part
still stands, but most of its imported boulders
lie strewn down the draw, all a testimony
to the labors of Cesario, Bernardo, and Juan,
and their mother and wives
unnamed.

The front room on Torres Street was the store,
the back room home. Built of large
adobe bricks, it seemed indestructible
here on this arid edge of the Chihuahuan Desert.

But one July
over fifteen inches of rain fell
on Langtry, rains that
had all the folks of town scurrying
to find pans and buckets to catch the leaks
from holes that may
have been there for decades—
who would have known?

And on Torres Street, what might
have lasted for centuries,
did not last the week.
One woman reported that
she heard a big boom and rushed outside

to see what had happened.
She thought it might be a car smash-up,
rare but not unheard of on the three
streets of Langtry.

She saw nothing. Later she learned
that the back room of the Torres House
had fallen in. Long hidden by mesquite
and cacti, the room could not have been
seen accidentally and now
not even by intention.

Then a few days later,
soundlessly, the front wall and its proud
J. P. TORRES fell across
Torres Street. Adobe crashed to dust,
taking its Texas Historical Marker with it.
Its old door poked out from the top of the heap
like parts of skeleton,
which it was.

Langtry men cleared the rubble off the street
and rescued the sign for repair—
repair and perhaps rewording:
"here stands" becomes "here once stood,"
like the Hall House across the street,
the Ice House down the block,
the cemetery, the barber shop,
the old Cantu place.

Things fall, we all know that,
they wear away, they break down.
In the abstract, "things change"
seems trite.

We are told that the Appalachian
mountains were once as tall
as the Alps. In Monument Valley,

thin red towers show the cores of
mountains. Floods create new
riverbeds and rivers dry up to become
rocky bush-filled arroyos.
We muse about time and finitude.

But in the concrete, in the adobe,
in Langtry, the falling of the Torres House
breaks our hearts.

Here of all places. Here where we have
found ten-thousand-year-old mammoth bones,
can still see four-thousand-year-old paintings
on shelter walls, discover frequently the stone
tools and fires of ancient hunter-gatherers.
Here we know nothing if we do not know time and change.

But the fall of the Torres Store is
hard to take, painful.
Old as it was, we took it for granted.
Monument to our history?
Symbol of the essence of Langtry, declaring
who we have been and who we are?

Yes, but, oh, so much more—
communal *and* intensely personal.
We grieve as we grieve
for ourselves, our families and the
artifacts that hold our story:
here we lived, worked, raised families,
suffered our daily vicissitudes,
here we prayed, watched for rain,
looked out for each other.

These things matter, are of essence.
Though they do not last, they count.
Vitality gone to dust,
breath gone to wind,
that's what makes our hearts ache.

Yet we are not inconsolable.
Our pain is strangely enlivening.
Deep in our bodies and souls,
we know we are part
of here and gone,
of time and beyond time.

5

In Just the Right Place

Insight is breakthrough [that] begins . . . with the cultivation of a
feeling for the unfamiliar, unparalleled, incredible. It is being involved
with a phenomenon, being intimately engaged to it, courting it.

Abraham Heschel, *The Prophets*

In Langtry, I would stand in a small clearing and say "Thou" to dog cactus and rocks, to vultures and clouds. I'm not sure it was what Buber meant but I think he would appreciate my intention. For him, intention mattered.

I would also say "Thou" to rock art images in shelters. That was harder because while I did not expect the cactus to answer back, I thought that the rock art might, or should.

Its silence was a personal failure.

November 19, 2005 Saturday

Yesterday was rough. It was dark and never got warm. I wrote some but have no idea how or if it fits into my project. I still can't make myself re-read what I have written.

Last night I went to Del Rio for Karen Aqua's presentation. She is an animator who showed four short films, the last about rock art, particularly that of the Three Rivers area in New Mexico. She had made paintings of the images and eventually got the idea for the film: *Ground Zero Sacred Ground.* It is a very powerful response to the first atomic testing. When I asked if the rock art images spoke to her, she replied that it was important to remember that these were sacred images not of her own culture. But I cannot help but think their power helped her find the idea for the film.

I did not sleep well, but I slept many times—in one-hour to two-hour segments—dreamed the FBI was investigating me for giving out abortion information. My mother was there. I don't have dreams that tell me about rock art and my project.

This morning is beautiful and I have the front door open. I lighted candles and put on *Silk Road,* the music of the nomads. I tried to do a meditation—imagined my inner dervish that loves this music.

Now I have to make my day, moment by moment. I'll write a reflection first. Just saw a pickup head out the Skiles' road. When I saw dust in the canyon, I thought someone was off on an adventure without me. I felt the same mix of emotions I have always had when I am left out—disappointment, righteous indignation, anger, loss— very physical feelings. I feel a bit better now because what I thought was dust was only the morning haze. I wonder if my friends here in Langtry know how badly I want to see more of this country! This morning I picked up Joseph Krutch's *The Desert Year.* Despite his somewhat elitist tone, I like his writing:

> In nature, one never really sees a thing for the first time until one has seen it for the fiftieth. It never means much until it has become part of some general configuration, until it has become not a "view" or a "sight" but an integrated world of which one is a part.

Krutch eschews what he calls "touring" but says that occasionally, though rarely, in a special place

> one experiences something like love at first sight. The
> desire to stay, to enter in, is not a whim or a notion
> but a passion. . . . If I do not somehow possess this, if
> I never learn what it was that called out, what it was
> that was being offered, I shall feel all my life that I
> have missed something intended for me. If I do not,
> for a time at least, live here I shall not have lived as
> fully as I had the capacity to live.

Early on, my fantasy, my dream was to head west. I have often imagined driving west from San Antonio with no plan just to see what would happen. When I arrived in California for school, I thought that was too far. This house in Langtry seems to be just the right amount of west. This is not my home country, since my roots lie in Big Spring and in my parents' Palo Pinto County. Yet here at my table looking out the front door east across canyons and hills at Mexico and at Guy and Vashti's rock house, I am in a world that calls me. I am in just the right place to contemplate the hunter-gatherers who painted here four thousand years ago. (I keep repeating the number in hopes that eventually I will understand it.)

I read that this was the one of the last places hunter-gatherers lived in North America. Almost everyone else had settled down into at least some kind of agriculture by the time the Europeans arrived. I wonder if they always had enough food here—just enough—and regretted leaving this beautiful ever-surprising land. Perhaps not. Maybe something else made them know it was time to move on.

A long, long time ago, in imaginable time, the Spaniards came through, right here. And Lipan Apaches were here, too. And now travelers on motorcycles with trailers pass by. They are all bundled up, leathers, gloves, all black. I know what that feels like—another way of exploring the day—wide-open and windy. At the highway they turn west—a long road no matter where they are headed.

I seem to be able to write and write—riding my computer down the day—watching the meadowlarks pecking away, a roadrunner darting past every once in a while. I looked it up in my bird book: "roadrunner *Geococcyx californianus*"—nowhere called a *chaparral* or *paisano*, its local names. I was going to describe it but can do no better than Ann Zwinger: "Each time it stops, its tail snaps up, its head swivels around for a sharp look, and seeing nothing of interest, off it bustles again, looking as if it has distant errands of great importance." The field guide reports that the paisano eats lizards and snakes and seldom flies. I have seen one fly a few feet to get off my path but never more than that.

I do not want it to eat my lizards and hope it finds no snakes nearby, but I really like its sudden, exciting dashes by. Ann Zwinger also notes that the roadrunner has been found in fossils dated 33, 000 years ago. How do I think about that? Which current flora and fauna have been here always? I have been told not much has changed except in times of more rain and more grass when bison came this far south for a while, and longer ago mammoths, and before that saber-toothed tigers and before, dinosaurs—right here.

I need someone with a pickup to take me down canyon roads. I don't want to rush it. I have a strong feeling that all will happen in just the right way, but I keep forgetting that I believe that.

Is this journal an exploration in itself? Perhaps.

Each morning I have been ferreting out an inspiring quote so here I go, personalizing Buber's *I and Thou*:

> Spirit in its human manifestation is a response of Mary Locke to her *Thou*. Mary Locke speaks with many tongues, tongues of language, of art, of action; but the spirit is one, the response to the *Thou* which appears and addresses her out of the mystery. Spirit is the word. . . . Spirit is not in the *I*, but between *I* and *Thou*. It is not like the blood that circulates in you, but like the air in which you breathe. Mary Locke lives in the spirit, if she is able to respond to her *Thou*. She is able to, if she enters into relation with her whole being. Only in virtue of her power to enter into relation is she able to live in the spirit.

I am trying to practice silence, to approach this place at least with imagination of "power to enter into relation." I imagine relationship with the place, the rock art, the folks of Langtry. It gives this whole experience importance, seriousness, potential, hope.

It is 11 a.m. and I am going to go for a walk. Shall I drive to the edge of the canyon and walk down to the river with my fishing pole or shall I walk all the way or only to the canyon—skip the pole? Who knows how many more warm days we will have, and the weather is perfect right now. I will make myself a picnic. But first I will make a calendar to show how many days before I have to send something to Chris.

Right There. Look.

Wind uncovers old bones,
fossils, stone tools,
every day.

Rain slips a layer
off of the canyon walls
and artifacts long buried
come into view.

Treasure exposed, however,
does not mean
treasure seen.

Jack told me about some immigrants
newly come across the Rio Grande.

They came to the house for food,
received bread and chicken
and left.

Soon the border patrol arrived—
searched high and low—
but never found them,
hide nor hair.

Yet they were right there,
only a few yards from the house.

It seems impossible that scrub brush
could hide a group of men and their dinner,
but it did, easily.

Either they were well-hidden or
the searchers had no imagination
for what was right there under their noses.

Jack told me that Native Americans
had left hundreds of small fire circles
on top of the canyon,
that I had walked over them every day.

How could that be?
I was always looking,
but I had no imagination
for ancient fire circles.
I saw only rock, dirt and rocks.
Then he pointed at the middle of the dirt road—
"Right there. Look."

Yes, now I see.
These rocks are different from the others—
intentional,
signs of ancient peoples.

But who would know,
who could see?

In the Shelter of Story

I

The stories of earlier people gave them
hope and meaning,
or so we like to imagine.
Now, when our own no longer suffice,
we look to their stories and lives
for reminders, for renewal,
as they, too, lived in the context
of their ancestors.

Were their stories of
hope and glory,
truth and justice,
dignity and grandeur,
love, imagination,
creativity, nobility—

or, alas, were these early folks
savages and not noble at all—
only primitive, fearful, greedy,
rough, crude,
wild and naked?
Likely they were like us,
always both.

Perhaps they were noble men and women
surviving by hunting small animals
and gathering plants, sharing
not only because they had to, but because
it was the right thing to do.

We can imagine that
and wish to be so lucky.
Imagining the human lot to be full
of splendid purpose—even though

eon after eon little changed.
Fall is different from spring,
but this fall the same as the last.

II

Purpose and hope—
I believe all people including
the people of the canyons
and rock art of the lower Pecos
need these.

I believe they hope for rain,
for food, for protection
from nature's vicissitudes.

III

I imagine all types of people doing all sorts
of things—reconcilers, rebels,
weak and strong
followers and leaders
singers and dancers
grinders and cooks
hunters, fishermen, weavers.

Storytellers, bards
sing the communal myth—
not merely the amazing thing
that happened on that day's hunt,
but the stories of their ancestors.

Beside the fire, the storyteller begins and,
if she is brave enough to let the images
lead, they may take her
into the darkness where figures
and movement are sensed
but not seen,

into a story beyond her own creativity
into Story itself.
She may be led by who knows what powers
into the unsayable,
into story great enough to hold all stories.

IV

The thing "darkly felt,"
primordial, unconscious
striving to be spoken—
how do we say it,
this unsayable thing?
We cannot, of course,
yet, ever doomed to fail,
we keep trying.

One trick of the storyteller is to offer up
images that do not quite make sense,
that are paradoxical, that contradict each other
and our own good reason.
But if teller and listeners are deep in the canyon
or desert or forest, the bizarre and surreal
do not seem out of place.
Listeners go along because they trust the bard,
and the singer keeps singing
because she trusts the story.

In the end, after all,
they sit in silence and linger
in the shadow of another world.

V

Eventually, of course, all must
leave the hearth,
but nothing is lost—
the experience of the story

makes them feel and know that existence,
their very own hunter-gatherer life,
has meaning and purpose.

In stories of gods forming
the world or of their own family traveling,
the numinous may shine
through and between the images.
Each telling new,
each story ancient.

White Shaman

Driving west, our caravan of trucks turns right and stops at a gate decorated with an iron cutout of a Pecos River Style shaman—or anthropomorphic figure, to be perfectly correct. The sign reads "White Shaman—The Rock Art Foundation." The gate-opening ritual here requires knowing the secret code for the padlock. Carolyn, our leader, knows it well, and we are in.

We navigate a pretty good two-track dirt road, at least good when it is dry as it is today. I think I know where we are headed because as always I have studied the map. If you turn right from west, you go north. The problem out here in west Texas is that the west-going road often goes north—and occasionally south. This ostensibly north-going road must negotiate canyon rims created by the river's meanders. When the truck stops at the picnic shelter and the outhouse, I look for the sun to see if west is still west—the direction of the nearby Pecos River. I find the sun shimmering beneath the clouds, but no river—only the flat top of a mesa and a few scrubby bushes.

We head off down the trail to the re-creation of an early Native American village. Steve and Brenda Norman have built shelters called "wickiups" and decorated them with antlers, bones, feathers, and a few woven baskets. A wickiup is made by bending branches or cane for a frame, tying it together, and covering it with brush. It has none of the glamour of a tipi or even of a cave shelter. Here where there is no natural shelter and little material to work with, the little brush dome looks like the habitat of the hopeful in a land of no hope. What protection would these scrawny branches be from wind and dust or rain? What privacy could it offer?

But when I crawl inside and sit alone with a basket in my hands, I realize that the circular interior of the wickiup feels secure, someone's place to be—her own home, though "sparse" is too ample, though "temporary" too solid to describe it. In the middle of the group of wickiups is a flat rock on top of which are scraps of chipped stone—the bane of the archaeologists who know that they were recently made in a demonstration but that for later visitors will be difficult to distinguish from the ancient ones.

As we continue down the trail, accepting on faith that the canyon is near, we receive our warnings and reminders: Do not pick up anything. Do not touch the plants because they will pierce and puncture and possibly sting. Watch out for snakes. Watch out for loose or slippery rocks on the trail.

If we had thought we were away from "civilization," we are disabused of that notion when we come to a box atop a post. There we sign our names and the date and time as well as the document to declare that we will not hold the Rock Art Foundation liable for disasters and mishaps. Thus we are reminded—if we had doubted— that current politic pushes deep into the wilderness.

We sign up and sign out, put the papers back in the box, pick up our walking sticks, turn onto the trail, and lo and behold! there is the canyon right in front of us, where only moments and a few feet before it had appeared that the mesa stretched unbroken for miles. This is just how this country is—nothing is quite what it seems.

The trail meanders and is variously smooth and rough, steep and level, clear and hidden. As with most of the trails out here, you can't see where you are going until you get there. Just when you think there will always be one more boulder or one more cactus to negotiate, you look up, and there it is—White Shaman shelter with its startling and thrilling images.

For long ages, people had to climb almost straight up the treacherous canyon wall to get into the cave, but now stairs lead up the last fifteen feet to the floor of White Shaman Shelter. Most of the floor is slanted and very slippery, but on the right is a flat, narrow ledge in front of the panel of pictographs. This shelter seems too small to have been lived in, but the paintings indicate that here something serious happened—the painting of the wall itself, of course, but there also must have been rites or ceremonies, praying, dancing, music-making. People came here to do much more than paint and look.

The cave is above an inlet of the Pecos and across the way is another shelter even less accessible. One woman said that once some of her group climbed down into that cave to drum so the others could hear and feel the sound reverberate at White Shaman. I study the far cliff and cannot figure out how anyone could get to that shelter, but I would like to try. I would like to feel the beat of the drums.

Looking at the rock art as Carolyn points out lines and dots, shamans and strange creatures, and patterns and motifs she discerned more clearly when she made her detailed copy of the mural, my mind wanders back to the days they were painted and to the days long after that when they marked this place in the canyons as special or sacred or numinous. I imagine a procession of people coming to this wall—those who understood its meaning, those who had stories to tell about its importance to them and to their ancestors, and many more just like me who don't know what it is or why it is here, only that it mattered, and it still does.

6

The Current Scene

Our bodies have formed themselves in delicate reciprocity with the manifold textures, sounds, and shapes of an animate earth—our eyes have evolved in subtle interaction with *other* eyes, as our ears are attuned by their very structure to the howling of wolves and the honking of geese.

David Abram, *The Spell of the Sensuous*

Rereading my Langtry stories, I was surprised by recurring themes of loss and death. Much of what I experienced evoked grief and regret. Imagined deaths of an archaic hunter triggered images of ancestors I never knew in cemeteries I never visited. Abandoned houses and abandoned shelters symbolized my own impermanence and mortality. One morning I recorded a dream in which my house fell apart. Later that day, I wrote about the fallen stones of the Torres house. It was much later that I saw the connection.

November 20, 2005 Sunday

I am always catching up with yesterday. I took off for my hike just a bit after noon.

But first, before writing about yesterday and before heading to Jack and Wilmuth's house for lunch, I want to describe this morning. I got up in time to sing and dance the sun up—it was 40 degrees but no wind and no clouds. Just as the sun was coming over the horizon, Jack drove up to invite me to church. So just before 8 a.m., I started down the road afoot when I heard a truck coming along behind me. In it were Brenda and Steve Norman, who gave me a short ride up the hill to the Langtry Baptist Church.

Joining us were the Skiles, Pete Billings and his daughter, Linda Billings, and Lou and Jackie Jones. Jackie played his guitar and led us in singing old songs from my childhood Sunday School. I was especially glad to sing "I love to tell the story." Together Jackie and Lou told the story about a country hymn written by Dottie Rambo and Jimmie Davis, a country singer and a former governor of Louisiana. Then they sang it. I couldn't believe my good fortune getting to hear it. Our preacher, Phil Dering, did a good, thoughtful job—a nice speaker.

After church, I visited a while with Jackie. He told me he smoked and drank until he got saved twenty-two years ago and was called to sing. He gave up his vices, his voice got better, and he has been playing the guitar and singing in churches ever since. He and Lou were headed to the 10 o'clock service in Comstock.

Jack asked if I wanted to do a couple of chores with him on the ranch and, of course, I was ready to go. When he got here, he said he had forgotten to tell me he had a live skunk in the back of the truck. They had caught it in a cage right by their house. He drove gingerly, and when we got just inside the gate of his west pasture, we stopped and Jack slowly lifted the trap out of the back of the pickup. I photographed as he removed the blue plastic cover and opened the door to let it free. It ran into the brush so quickly that I am not sure I caught it in any of my pictures, but it left without spraying us, so I decided that was my good omen for the day.

Jack showed me where the Chinese railroad builders had camped when they were laying the rails east from Los Angeles back in the

1800s. The track was for the southern route of the Southern Pacific Railroad. He showed me the rock circle they had used to hold the big wok he found there. I found a piece of blue and white Chinese pottery—probably a rice bowl. It is so strange to imagine teams of Chinese workers out here in this rugged desert land far, far, from China.

On the other side of the Pecos, laying the Galveston, Harrisburg, and San Antonio track from the east were mostly Irish, Italian, and German workers. Around their camps many, many beer bottles are strewn still. The east track and west track met right here. There are pictures of officials hammering in the final gold spike. The train went right through downtown Langtry.

We drove right on the old rail track (ties and rails long removed)—deep straight cuts through hills. Jack said he was told that they carried the dirt out in baskets—I try to picture that. We also looked at a little rock bridge over a culvert. The rock work is very beautifully done—carved with much more attention to design than necessary—pride of the stoneworker for work to be seen by few except critters.

Then we went to a place overlooking the Rio Grande—just the spot where he and his granddaughter caught a forty-four pound catfish, the head of which is on a post of his fence. It is shockingly huge. He pointed out shelters where there is rock art and the big overhang where his younger son proposed to the woman to whom he is now married. She said yes, and she also said she would never again climb up into that cave. The shelter (one of the Twin Caves) is high on the side of a steep cliff. I couldn't see how anyone could get up there or any floor to stand on once they did.

After lunch of home-made venison stew with Jack and Wilmuth, Jack showed me his artifacts. He said lots of people (many are scientists) come out here to study his collection, most gathered long ago from railroad and Native American sites. I was most drawn to the weavings—mats, shoes, baskets, fishing and rabbit nets—all so carefully and beautifully made. I could feel the gesture of the weaver in the turn of the thread. Jack said because he has lived here where the early hunters lived and thought about them and their lives so much, he has a strong relationship with them. (His and Wilmuth's house sits right on top of Eagle Nest shelter.)

Jack does not believe these people were nomads but thinks they probably stayed here year around. In one shelter on his land there are over ten feet of ashes and detritus (centuries of fires). We talked about burials. The ones he has seen have been in the shelters where the people lived. The body would be covered with a mat and, if it were a woman, a *matate* or grinding bowl might be placed on top.

I asked Jack about the sinkhole burial at Seminole Canyon, which he knew about because he had provided the ladder for the exploration. The story goes that, on land the state of Texas bought from the Zuberbueler family for the park, there was a wide area with nothing on it but one big flat rock which an archaeology graduate student thought seemed out of place. When they lifted the stone, they found an opening about two feet wide. That is when they went to Jack for the ladder he had used for spelunking.

The archaeologists dropped down a narrow passage for about seven feet and then came into a cavern. Directly below the opening was a mound that contained human bones, some of which had been burned. There was also an older mound where they found a spear point over seven thousand years old.

A report for the Texas Archaeological Survey included the opinion that "the dead were rather summarily disposed of by simply dropping the corpse down this convenient sinkhole." The people were likely dead before they were "cast into the cavern" and that this was a "single or short-lived practice." The presence of projectile points might point to a violent death, but the actual cause of the deaths could not be discerned.

We do not have a theory, but we have a story, and a sad one, or so we might guess—just tossing the body of your family member or friend into a "convenient sinkhole." The truth is that we don't know what happened there—but I would love to see that place.

When I left Jack and Wilmuth's, I drove over to Pump Canyon. It is very deep and frightening. I did not go to the very edge but sat back from it. I could see the place on the canyon wall where there used to be a very long steep staircase that the railroad built when they got water here—thus "Pump Canyon." When they no longer needed the water, they burned the stairs—afraid folks would fall down and break their necks, I assume.

I sat on a ledge where that canyon opens on to the Rio Grande and my telephone rang! That is one of the only places where I can get a signal. It was Tom. I knew if he were here, he would scare me by getting too close to the edge. Later at the store, I was told a young man had fallen off the cliff there. The story goes that he was drunk and peeing when a big wind came up.

Heading back to town, I stopped by the cemetery. All different kinds of fences surround plots of one or two graves, many of the gravestones or wooden crosses fallen and illegible. A jumble of graves, all facing east. It is sad in a way, but sweet also. Within a fenced area are buried Jack's parents, Guy and Vashti. (At first, I pronounced it to rhyme with "wash-tee" but learned it rhymes with "dash-tie"—it's from the Bible.)

Went over to the other side of Eagle Nest Canyon to say goodbye to the sun. I had sung it up, so I had to *namaste* it down. All quiet, no animals, lots of mosquitoes, of course. Earlier Jack had pointed up to what may have been an eagle. He said sometimes they come here for the winter.

So now it is dark and I am getting blue. I look toward the highway at the three old buildings which have a new importance for me because Guy Skiles built them—two stores and a very sweet two-unit tourist court. I have a very tender place in my heart for anybody who has enough faith and courage to open a store.

I was surprised to learn that the odd assortment of tin buildings here beside my house are the creations of an unusual man—a scientist/environmentalist or an eccentric, depending on who you ask. There is a half-built Conestoga wagon atop an old car chassis, a tin A-frame, something that looks like a chicken house and an old trailer with a tin building around it. They say he put solar heating in his outhouse—very ahead of his time.

When I stopped by the store and post office today, a woman came by to inquire about any house that might be for sale here. There are only about five habitable houses, a couple more that might be rebuilt, and the rest are beyond repair. The store owner, who has been here for thirty-three years and whose husband is from here, said emphatically, "There is nothing for sale in Langtry. Lots of people want land here, but no one will sell." She had a tone of "we don't need any newcomers in these parts," which would seem less strange if there were more old-timers. Wonder how much of an outsider I am to them. (Jack told me he told someone they were renting their house to a writer. I thought, "Really? Who?" and then realized it was me!)

So that is today.

Yesterday when I walked to the river, I scared up a bunch of wild hogs and they scared me back up the road. I had seen two walking through the brush in the canyon—for a minute I was sure one was a mountain lion because it was big and brown. It reminded me again of Africa and seeing the slight movement of creatures emerging from the brush. I enjoyed watching them until I realized their trail went down into the canyon and back up to right where I was eating my sandwich. I left in a timely fashion.

It is 6:17 p.m. and I am not going to write anymore tonight. I wish I thought this were a dissertation. But I do love being here. I can't wait for Tom to come.

Good night and good luck.

Death and Stories

I

No one knows much about
these people we refer to as
ancient ancestors of primordial times,
nomadic hunters and gatherers.
They left no words,
only art and artifacts.

Yet our ancestors are with us—
in blood and bones, in memory,
nearer than that, in stories
of today's happenings,
of hopes for tomorrow,
of endings, beginnings, amazements.

II

A daily event—a death
the story of how he died.
Tell me that story.

> *He awoke as he always did—picked up*
> *his hunting tools and headed off down the trail.*
> *It was sunny that morning, hot, no clouds.*
> *We men all left together,*
> *but he chased something up the canyon—*
> *must have been something big,*
> *a rabbit, maybe. Then, right where the small*
> *creek goes around the bluff,*
> *it happened.*
>
> *A huge boulder came down on him.*
> *We heard it hit and his scream.*
> *He was dead by the time we got there.*
> *It took us a long time to roll the boulder*
> *so we could bring him home.*

That's how he died, the immediate story.
There is another, broader story:

> *He was always the kind of man to go off alone*
> *without telling anyone. He was quiet*
> *and he was brave.*
> *We will miss this good hunter.*
> *Now we will all have to work harder*
> *to get enough food.*

And a bigger story yet:

> *The gods were angry,*
> *because we did not make the proper offering,*
> *because gods get angry for no good reason,*
> *because gods demand sacrifice,*
> *because gods are dangerous and unpredictable.*

I do not know how people of these canyons
made sense of death.
I doubt we are any better at it.
It is too shocking—
at breakfast, someone tells their dreams
and by nightfall they are gone.
The body will stay until disposed of,
but the man or woman or child we knew,
gone.

III

All die, of course, and sometimes we eat them—
the deer, rabbit, snake, mouse,
and even so, each time breath goes out and
does not return,
we are mystified. How can it be?
What kind of world is this?

I invented this story—a hunter-gatherer
of the Pecos River, of the painted walls,
dies in a rock fall.
But it might have happened.
Goodness knows there are enough boulders
scattered all over the canyons.
In thousands of years of falling,
someone probably had been hit.

I do not know what these folks thought
about the gods and their anger
or unpredictability or love.
It is a mystery why the gods act,
but a fact that they do.
Who knows? Perhaps that hunter,
in the crashing of the rock, became
a god himself.

IV

I do know that when there is a death,
a story is told and it helps.
My young friend Betsy, a talented violinist,
jumped off of a building in Brooklyn.
For weeks, her friends and family had
gatherings and memorials where
they told many Betsy stories.

In Texas, I mourned alone. I could not recover.
I did not understand how those who were closer to her
did not seem as inconsolable as I.

Then one day her roommate Rona came to see me.
She told me about Betsy's depression and misery,
of her desire for relief.
Rona did not speak of gods directly
but she acknowledged an underlying mystery—
Betsy's suicide as part of a larger story we accept

without understanding.
Rona left and I was able to move on,
to get back into life.

V

I cannot imagine it was otherwise for the survivors
here in the Chihuahuan desert thousands of years ago.
Surely they, as I, wished things were different,
that their loved one were here cooking,
playing with the children, telling stories.

Yet I wonder if they,
living in small groups in shelters
of rocks or of reeds,
always feeling the wind and frost,
rain and hail,
surviving by killing,
and dying of unknowable causes,
did not know more of death.

VI

On good days a mouse or rabbit breathed, struggled,
died and was eaten—
no momentous event, a necessary death even,
but death nonetheless.

I do not kill my sheep,
my chickens or cows,
do not witness their deaths.

Seldom have I suffered loss of friends or relatives.
My trips to the cemetery are infrequent,
but my grandmothers, Maggie and Anna,
knew well the way to the burial ground.

They walked the path, accompanying caskets
of parents, sisters, brothers, husbands, babies.
Maggie lost four—her first-born Edward,
ten-year-old Willie Mae, whose appendix ruptured,
and the twins, Margaret, dead at birth,
and Elizabeth, eight days later.

Maggie never recovered and died herself soon after.
Anna buried her first-born twin and another twin later.
I look at the dates. Maggie's twins died only weeks after
her father-in-law and her sister.
At McAdams Cemetery on the Brazos River,
those mounds were still fresh when
Maggie came with her twin daughters.
The path to the cemetery was well-worn but never easy.

VII

I'm not saying it was less miserable
for them or for those living on the Pecos River long ago,
but they could not have been shocked,
as I am, with each confrontation with death.
Might they have accepted death
as natural, like the rain?
Is that possible?

Depredation Fighter

The man looked bigger than life when he stood up in front of the thirteen year olds to tell of his work. He *is* bigger than life. Tom Glasscock is the Val Verde County agent in charge of problems of depredation. He is tall, wears a huge worn brown Stetson and a large silver rodeo champion belt buckle which lies horizontal under his stomach. He spoke low in a monotone. I was worried that the students could not hear him well, but my husband said that it was enough that these young people know someone like him exists in this world of high technology and advanced science.

Tom is called out when ranchers have problems with cats or coyotes (which he pronounces in one syllable, "cyotes") killing their livestock. The rest of the time he searches over the range looking for varmints. But contrary to what one might think upon first meeting Tom, his main mission is to teach and cajole ranchers to live with the natural fauna of this eastern Chihuahuan desert habitat.

He told about a contractor developing a new neighborhood right over an old cat trail. The cats he is referring to are cougars and bobcats. He said that, in contrast to coyotes, cats do not change their habits and walking this trail was an ancient habit for them. Not long after families moved into the new houses, they began to report with alarm that something had killed their dogs. "First of all," Tom said, "if the cat killed Rover, he wasn't a very good dog anyway."

Tom is trying to teach us that the animals have done a good job accommodating humans while humans have done a poor job of accommodating animals. "Why," he asked, "don't road builders make overpasses so animals can move about without getting killed by vehicles?"

Tom is a great admirer of the intelligence and cunning of the coyote. Coyotes eat meat when meat is available and are vegetarians when it is not. Coyotes survive on the prairie and in the streets of Los Angeles.

To illustrate the way some animals help each other, Tom told about the coyote and the badger. When the coyote smells a skunk, he does not run away but rather comes running toward the smell, because he thinks there is a good chance that a badger has killed the skunk and the coyote can mooch some supper. In fact, hunters use skunk aroma to lure coyotes because they can catch the scent from over two miles away.

Tom Glasscock grew up in this country in the little town of Juno on the Devils River. He was a bull rider and became a rodeo producer which means he provided the horses and bulls for the rodeo. He met his wife Glendell in rodeo circles as she was a barrel racer (not chasing barrels but racing around them on specially trained horses).

When he arrived at camp, I asked if he had met any skunks that day—human or otherwise. He said he had, but they decided to leave each other alone, contrary to the previous day's encounter with a rattlesnake. Tom almost stepped on it and, as it was a "him or me" situation, Tom killed him.

Pump Canyon

Eagle Nest Canyon

Kelly Cave, Skiles Cave, and Twin Caves

Torres Store and Home

Anthropomorphs at Halo Shelter

Curly Tail Panther on Devils River

Mary Locke, Pete, Catfish

Jack and Wilmuth Skiles

7

Core and Chaos

[Myths] represent situations in which boundaries have been crossed from unconsciousness to consciousness, innocence to experience, natural to cultural, chaos to order. . . . Myths are a means by which humans attempt to integrate themselves with the contradictions of their human, natural, and supernatural worlds. By concentrating on life-and-death matters, myths help humans become graceful enough to dance, to leap, and to linger in ritual meant to promote life.

Christopher Vecsey, *Imagine Ourselves Richly*

Myths are the stories humans tell to make sense of the world, to remember their origins, to illuminate the purpose of life and to limn rules for sustaining it. It is the nature of these stories to emerge from life and to shape life. In a hunter-gatherer group of about fifteen, the size that could sustain itself in the Lower Pecos, each and all owned the stories of the past as well as those that held promise for the future.

November 21, 2005 Monday

It is 5:30 a.m.—I just spread all my papers on the bed. I dipped into my journal entry for November 29, 2004—just a year ago: "The question is, can the story of my doing the dissertation be part of the dissertation?" Today I would have to say, "Yes!"

My life in Langtry:

sky clouds stars sun moon Milky Way sunrise

sunset rocks shrubs fossils snakes spiders bees

My life is outside. Even when I am working in the house, I go out every little bit to check the sky—clouds by day and stars by night—and the land—any creatures moving? Birds, bugs, porcupine, deer, wild hogs, wild goats, Border Patrol?

I have too many loose threads. Tom says, "You have to find your core, your grabber." I'm trying! Is it my journey west? My journey to myself? (Whatever *that* means!) I want a revelation.

I brought the sun up at 7:15 a.m. from the house. It was not good enough to merely look out the window, so I opened the door to look through the screen. But even the screen between me and the sun seemed like too much of a barrier, so I kept running outside and then running back in (because it was cold—thirty-nine degrees).

I fixed a very big breakfast and now it is 8:08 a.m. I have been up four hours and I'm dragging. But I am sorting papers right and left and up and down. I cannot go anywhere until I have some sort of list—searching for my CORE!

Can I find my core in dreams? Last night I dreamed that Carolyn Boyd was doing an archaeological project on another planet. You had to go there on a spaceship and then take a treacherous journey to where she was. Then you had to be accepted into the program.

I traveled to the planet with scientists who were very nervous about their qualifications—about knowing enough science. I was not worried because I was not even trying to be a scientist and, even though I had to go through the approval process, I knew I would be accepted because my qualification was *love*. I knew love. They needed me and they knew it.

Also I was watching for someone whom I was sure would show up—the just-right man, a particular man. I saw one I thought was he but then immediately realized it was not.

So, a dream about my work at last. I find it encouraging, of course. But what has love got to do with it?

Surely We Are Kin

I

If these rock art images were more
familiar, less bizarre, I might study
them to seek meaning.
Because they are strange and seemingly
indecipherable,
my eyes move quickly away
to the sky, the rocks, the river,
and eventually, inevitably,
I turn to my mind's eye.

I think about traveling with the people
who lived in these canyons.
Even though their art tells me no story,
their journey seems familiar,
desirable even.

Like them, I trample over these mesas
and canyons, dodge swooping vultures,
am attacked by cactus, surprised by turkeys,
burnt by the sun and battered by the wind.
This place, their place, is becoming
my natural habitat,
my home.

II

The yearning I carry
began under the open skies
of West Texas where I grew up.
The days were unclouded,
the horizon clear and distant,
always pulling.
The west was my heart's desire,
exotic and full of promise.

On west US 80 in Big Spring, a sign in front
of my house said: *El Paso: 300 miles*
and I imagined moving on—
New Mexico, Arizona, California,
Pago Pago, Hong Kong, Mongolia,
the Silk Road, Shanghai,
Shangri-La.

III

My imagination for the west
is sister to my imagination of
hunter-gatherers of the lower Pecos River.
They followed the bison south,
and when the bison headed back north,
they stayed.
Lord knows why,
unless it was the water, the canyons,
cool shade and incredible beauty.

Surely some places were better in the winter,
others in the summer.
Maybe right here in Eagle Nest Canyon
they found all they needed.

Did they look forward to the next move,
did they make each place home?
Were they like us—arranging their things to
mark their space—making beds and burials,
always reorienting—
Is the water up? Are the springs still running?

They must have met up with other family groups
to share food and stories and sons and daughters.

Did they have some stories for the children
and others children were not allowed to hear?

Did they sit by the fire and recall legends
of the long walk from the north or the south—
the first journeys of ancestors or gods?

Perhaps one tale began with
Long ago, when I was just a little girl
about your age, we were living in
the shelter that got no sun.
One morning, just as we were waking up . . .

Another: *See that coyote over there?*
His great-grandfather was a sly one! Back
when coyotes could talk . . .

IV

What kind of monsters filled their dreams?
There were plenty enough things to fear—
snakes, poisonous plants, the sun, and the rain.

Surely, with thousands of years of travel,
there were graves all along the trail
and each cliff held its tales of trouble,
triumph, death.

Remembering ancient times
or the last time,
loss here, discovery too,
a new person joined here,
celebration, music, dance,
ceremonies and burials,
the night the drummers continued on
through the storm.

Stories of horrible things
they could not hide or hide from—
what fears filled their souls,
what joy, what love?

V

Did all your women menstruate together?
Was there no shame about bodies,
male, female
young, old, budding, withering
about weakness or slowness
simple-mindedness?
Illnesses, deformities,
things worse than death?

Did you hate your mother and fear your father
or the other way around or neither?
Were there men who loved men
and women who loved women,
women who did men's chores
and men who worked with the women?

The deadly sins we know so well: greed
sloth, jealousy, envy, murderous rage,
did you know those?

VI

Like me, were you thrilled
when you saw signs of other people?
Anticipation, intrigue, curiosity—
perhaps someone dropped a basket
or lost a sandal.
What if it were a strange design
never seen before?
Might other people be nearby?
Mother, wife, husband, brother,
everyone—come here and look!
What do you think?

Signs of nature—though crucial—
are not as compelling, not so full of story,
as an old scraper or point.
A bone or fossil may be interesting,
but something made, touched, left
by another person—a world opens.

VII

Who spoke to you who
does not speak to us,
how did you pray,
for what did you hope?

that the child would get well,
that you would find food and water,
that soon you would get to
the place you loved the most,
that the other family would return
and your lover stay when they left?

If everything was the same
always the same,
perhaps your hopes were
bound in the day—
hope to find food,
hope for rain, or no rain,
hope for the daily safety,
hope against catastrophe,
a horrible death,
an impossible birth.

Hope that the gods will be kind,
cure, provide nourishment—
is that all?
Let my daughter be well,
let us have enough to eat today,
is that all?

Though I strain to enter into your world,
I know I cannot, even in my wildest imagination,
but I also cannot imagine life,
yours or mine, without hope.
In this, surely, we are kin.

Rivers and Threads

My journey—a road, a way, a path—
Whoa! not so fast!
It does not work that way for me—
far too straight.
I am many pieces going and coming
many different directions.

I traverse tributaries
of a yet unknown river,
hold threads not yet woven.
But even these images seem too hopeful,
as if the river or the weaving were
a given or a promise.

I imagine ideas radiating from my head
as in some of the rock art—
wavy lines shooting from an almost-
human's almost-head.

However I imagine it,
whatever metaphor I conjure
to understand my journey,
I long for one simple thought,
one beautiful thread,
one sparkling creek.

8

Sorting and Gleaning

Reciprocity [is] the ongoing interchange between my body and the entities that surround it. . . . Whenever I quiet the persistent chatter of words within my head, I find this silent or wordless dance always already going on—this improvised duet between my animal body and the fluid, breathing landscape that it inhabits.

David Abram, *The Spell of the Sensuous*

Besides sight and sound, other senses add to the synaesthesia of a person and a place—smell, taste, touch. Here in West Texas, the rocks, plants, insects, reptiles with their variety of sharp edges, thorns, and scales call to be touched and sometimes reach out to touch under their own power. Cacti, like scorpions and snakes, can attack, can hide and ambush. The wind and sun also touch, and the boundary of human skin offers little protection or separation.

November 22, 2005 Tuesday

3 p.m. I worked all day yesterday and all day today getting my papers sorted and working on my outline for the theory. I felt really good when I finished and took a shower and got dressed. It is too hot to walk right now, so I'll do some catching up.

Yesterday I went up the hill to use the telephone and came back by the eagles' nest. I saw what I thought might be an eagle. Pete Billings, who was working by the road, said there had been no eagles here in years, though Jack had told me they show up occasionally.

Pete told me about his family. His wife Dorothy died a few years ago of colon cancer. They had been married over sixty years. Both grew up in Langtry, children of Southern Pacific section foremen— one in charge of so many miles east and one of so many miles west. They were next-door neighbors. When Pete retired from his job as an engineer on the Southern Pacific (SP), he wanted to come back here (from Del Rio). So he told his wife if she would come to Langtry, he would build her a rock house on the cliff overlooking canyons of the Rio Grande. And she did and he did.

He confirmed that you cannot buy land here. The Dodd family owns most everything and does not want to sell in pieces. I heard they once listed the whole town on eBay for a million dollars. That could be an urban legend, or rural legend.

So that was my outing yesterday, except for a sunset walk to the canyon. I was really tired since I had been up since 4 a.m. I ate salad for supper, watched *Harry Potter*, and listened to basketball.

After working all day with my papers, sorting and gleaning, I was my most depressed last night—embarrassed that I had come here to do something I cannot do. I vaguely remembered that mornings were better so I just cursed a bit and went to bed.

This process reminds me of Psyche and her jobs: sorting grains, retrieving the golden fleece from the bushes, collecting elixir from the high mountain stream, and then going down to Hades for the beauty treatment. If I am still at the sorting stage, imagine the gleaning, retrieving, and descending I have to look forward to!

I love this thought of Giuseppe Tucci quoted by Thomas Merton in his *Asian Journal*: "Every shape and form that arises in the soul, every link which, in a mysterious way, joins us to the Universal Life and unites us, maybe without our being aware of it, to [our] most ancient experience, the voices which reach us from the depths of the abyss, all are welcomed with almost affectionate solicitude."

I wonder, just where is this arising of images in my soul? Is it only in dreams? Is it in my imagining the first civilization here? In my most personal experience—coming up from the depths (or canyon)? How can I unite with the hunter-gatherers without knowing it? And if I don't know it, does it matter? I do love the idea, the possibility of joining with universal life and the most ancient experience, if the voices will come on up from the depths of the abyss and not make me go down there to get them!

Tom comes tomorrow for Thanksgiving. I will be glad to see him and for him to see this place. Okay—today has not been eventful, but I did see an Amtrak go by headed west—as trains have been doing in these parts since 1883.

Devils River Panther

Climbing up the trail, I look no
farther than the feet of the woman
in front of me. I try to step exactly where
she steps. When we stop to catch
our breath, I look up the canyon
and see looming just ahead
the larger-than-life burnt orange panther
painted long years ago in this shelter
overlooking the Devils River.
I am shaken, stunned, weak-kneed.
This is not what I had expected.

The trail has been difficult and
the last part dangerous—a very
narrow ledge across a steep slick
slant, the river far below.
When I reach the overhang shelter,
I fall to the ground and hold on,
grateful for gravity.

I think I am ready to face the panther
now directly above me,
but again it knocks me off balance.
All around the panther body, its hair
is standing straight up—
my hair is doing the same.

I get my bearings
and begin to notice feline details:
tail swung wide over its back, open
mouth, sharp teeth, powerful
legs stretched backward.

I absorb the whole panther.
Suddenly, it breathes and naturally
I breathe with it.

Relief at Last

I tromp down the trail once again,
but with new hope.
I am eager to reach the puzzle—
"Let me at those enigmatic figures!
This time I will decode them."
I march armed with clear purpose—
not to commune but to explain.

How quickly the worm does turn.
When I reach the shelter and look at the rock art,
I am immediately uncomfortable,
hot, thirsty, afraid of falling,
confused and frustrated.
Nothing I see
makes a bit of sense.

I glance at the paintings
and then turn to something more familiar—
birds flying into crevices high on the cliff,
bees astir in a hive that reaches through
the shelter roof to the mesa above,
a huge oak tree washed downstream in the flood.

Finding the rock art images in
a book of watercolors
painted here sixty years ago,
I am able to make out
the turkey and the turtle.
Reading the book is much easier than
reading the wall.

Then, leaning back to look higher up,
I am stunned to see a huge creature
looming over me,
strange, bizarre, unsettling.

Moving upstream I find
tiny stick figures that look more like
mineral seeps than human art.
What is the story here?

At a loss, I wander downstream around the
fallen tree and there right in front of me
is the painting of a feline,
tail over its back, claws outstretched.

I relax—
finally I'm getting somewhere,
at long last something familiar.
I know cats.

9

Strangers from Home

Meaning is not in things but in between; in the iridescence, the interplay; in the interconnections; at the intersections, at crossroads. . . . In iridescence is flux, is fusion, subverting the boundaries between things; all things flow.

Norman O. Brown, *Love's Body*

It is one thing to read about Pleistocene fauna and another to discover that every rock on a hillside was once a sea creature. It is one thing to study the nomadic existence of hunter-gatherers and another to walk their trails to shelter and to river.

It is one thing to read historical facts of Langtry and another to float down the river with Pete pointing out sites of adventures eighty years ago and telling stories of trappers who were old when he was young. Reading signs is much more than identifying cacti, birds, and snakes.

It is a practice of meeting and response.

November 23, 2005 Wednesday Woden's Day

A late start today because I did not sleep more than two hours in a row. So I slept extra segments. Another incredibly exquisitely beautiful morning. I can see the blue and green glass insulators sparkle on the fence at Guy and Vashti's.

I worked all day yesterday and did not even go for a walk. At four I drove up to the filling station to use the telephone and then drove on up the road that appears to be an oil-field road—well maintained but nothing on it. I am sure it leads to ranches, but it somehow does not look like a ranch road—too generic. At the top of every hill, I saw only more hills and more road. I turned around to drive back toward the canyons—that's more fun.

Then I decided to go to the Pecos. Thinking I *might* go fishing, I had brought my old chicken carcass. I saw a wonderful huge hawk on an electric post. I stopped right under it and watched for a long time. It did not bother about me at all.

At the river, only one other person, a fisherman. I looked around and decided to fish for a minute but realized I had not brought my purse—no fishing license, no driver's license. Besides that, the fish likely would not prefer old cooked chicken to the fisherman's fresh chicken livers. So I headed on home to watch the sunset.

I did go for a short walk behind the house and saw my critter of the day—a small armadillo. It waddled away—a few steps and stop—a few more and stop—and on into the bushes. The sunset is wonderful—the best golden pink is just before dark. I cannot see far west because of a hill, but the color was brilliant over the eastern canyon. I kept trying to go inside—it got chilly the moment the sun went down and the mosquitoes found me—but I could not leave. Every second, the light changed and the colors moved west.

The nights are long and strange. I watched more *Harry Potter* as I ate my chicken noodle soup. After some solitaire, I made tea and turned out all the lights and watched the trucks go by. Soon several trains came around the bend. One sat on the tracks a long time and then took off like the Polar Express with its three bright lights illuminating the rail. When trucks were along side, I could only see the top of the train, and it did seem like a ghost train—the only way I could tell it was still moving was the rattle of the window.

Except for trucks and trains, it is almost completely quiet here. At dusk I do not want to come in because the nights are long and also I am not sleeping well.

Now it is 7:08 p.m. I am waiting for Tom.

I worked some today. Generally, I read and take notes and then hunt around for rocks and broken glass. I found a burner top from a stove and made a mandala with colored glass.

Went to the canyon to call Tom to see where he was. No answer. I stopped by the Billings' for homemade ice cream and Pete showed me great old pictures of the first Pump Canyon steps. He said he will go fishing with me if I get the bait. Showed me pictures of a really, really creepy 150-pound alligator gar. It is a fish but its head looks exactly like an alligator's. It was as tall as Pete. He shot it to bring it in—a funny way to fish. Jack said there are a lot here in the river. I hope never to see one face to face!

Went again to the top of the hill and this time I did get Tom who was just approaching Uvalde—2 1/2 hours away and a long wait for me. I had just gotten home when Jack came by to ask if I wanted to go on a picnic about sunset. Of course I said YES! He and Wilmuth and their daughter Peggy, a teacher in Big Spring, picked me up and we went to Twin Canyons. The vista in the dusky light was beautiful. We were overlooking the *vega* (new word: a thicket of brush and trees at edge of river). Mosquitoes, but fun nevertheless.

Jack stood looking out over the Rio Grande to the cliffs on the other side and said he was thinking of the old Mexican woman he found dead in one of the caves. She had shown up across the river from Langtry one day, and the people of town took her food even though the Border Patrol told them not to. He said she was sort of crazy—she said she was going to walk to her daughter's place in Chicago although she had no idea where Chicago was. It was Christmas when Jack found her—she had been dead about a month. From what he could see of her stuff, all she had had to eat when she died was some lemon rind and a piece of gum that had been chewed over and over. We just stood and looked at the cave, remembering and imagining.

I asked about the early Langtry families. He said that one in particular was really rough. The story is told that they would hire people to work for them and then, when it came time to pay the wages, the workers would mysteriously disappear. Where was Judge Roy Bean when they needed him!

So now it is almost 7:30 p.m. When I got home from the picnic, I smelled a skunk right here—close. I don't mind it really, smells like the country to me.

I can't quite imagine how it will be to have Tom and Montana [our Llasa apso] and Hector [our tabby cat] here with me. I have mixed emotions about having the animals here. It is strange to have even Tom. Such a small little world I have made for myself. Completely quiet—just me and my thoughts. But you can go crazy like that. I didn't talk to anyone at all yesterday except the fisherman. I haven't been to E. J.'s store or Mike's filling station in a while. I now know seven of the twelve people of Langtry. I hope Tom can meet them.

I'll close and get my thoughts straight for company. Life's rich pageant!

Good night and good luck.

Many Rivers to Cross

On a border, the sides
differ in some way
or no border.
A border is created by naming.
A line is drawn and differences
hitherto unnoticed
now appear obvious and essential.

Here on my table is *Border Healing Woman*:
Pat Ellis and Jewel Babb tell the story of Jewel,
a healer at Indian Hot Springs,
where she relieved suffering,
inner and outer, mental and physical,
where boundaries abound
and passages are hidden.

Jewel's border was the Rio Grande
southeast of El Paso, where the river
barely trickles in the rainy season
and dries up in the dry
but a border nonetheless—
Texas in the United States of America on the north
and Chihuahua, "south of the border down Mexico way,"
as the song goes.

Not all of the Rio Grande
can be navigated
for the reason just stated—no water,
and for reasons rumored—
border guards, some official,
some self-appointed, and renegades—
selling, carrying, using
drugs and guns.

You might cross the *Rio Bravo*
by bridge at the guarded gates
or by wading or swimming—no problem finding
a low water crossing.

When I was growing up, I heard a lot about
crossing a river, the *Brazos de Dios*,
and the floods that isolated ranches for weeks at a time.
At the First Baptist Church in Big Spring, we sang
about gathering at the river, about crossing Jordan,
about the river that flows by the throne of God—
the same one that flowed into the baptistry
from the painting that hung above it,
or so I imagined.

And one day, I would cross over, cross the threshold
between life here and life on the other side.
I imagined my parents, Fred and Ellen,
my grandparents whom I never knew,
my aunts, Lee Ella, Eula Kate and Willie Mae,
and Uncle Bob, murdered on the streets of Mineral Wells,
welcoming me across.

I don't remember what song gave me that picture—
maybe it was just my mother.
Now, no matter how much I give up Heaven,
I can't quite get rid of coming to that river
where my loved ones wait to celebrate my crossing.

But today, I think, is not that day
and for now my river is the Rio Grande,
a border and no border at all.
Water wall and water passage
for body and for soul.

Ten in the Evening

I was alone, working my puzzle
all the doors and windows open
to the April wind—too strong to let in
and too luxurious to close out.
A train went by, its big light
searching west.

Then a pickup stopped on the road
just past my house.
It backed up and pulled forward
but not into my driveway.

Forward and back, again and again,
not straight, but weaving.
I could not imagine what was happening
but it alarmed me.
I dialed my friend's number,
I did not press "Talk,"
but I was ready.

Then someone—a man—climbed out of the truck
and called to the house
(I was standing to the side of the screen door,
watching):
"I just ran over a big snake on the road—
a diamondback."
Later I realized it was not "snake" or "big"
that made me shudder but "diamondback,"
a rattler with its tales of death.

I walked out—barefoot—with my flashlight.
The man had his door open,
its light just enough to see where he pointed
at a coil, a labyrinth of snake
and more blood and guts than a snake should have.

It had crawled off of the road,
crawled and curled to die.
We thought it was dead anyway.
We had no stick to prod it
and were standing back,
taking no chances.

"It was headed straight for your house,"
a woman's voice came from the pickup.
"He said, 'There's a snake on the road,' and
I said, 'Well, kill it!'"

The sight of the familiar diamond pattern
and the thought of its coming to my house,
the thought of stepping out my door
onto this snake
gave me chill bumps all over.

I was glad to have been saved,
but it seemed tragic, too,
for all the reasons you can imagine.

Just now, I hurried outside
to see it in the morning light.
I wore shoes and carried a stick.

But it was gone.
I found where it had been,
but nothing remains.

In the night, a herd of javelina
came into the yard to eat birdseed.
Do they eat rattlesnakes?
Were huge vultures swooping here
in the dark?
Something came and left
only blood on the rocks.

Wait—two vultures are here now
circling right by my door,
black, huge, powerful.
For them, the snake's death
was no tragedy
but midnight manna.

10

Thanksgiving Tales and Trails

The past is not simply "received" by the present. The present is "haunted" by the past and the past is modeled, invented, reinvented, and reconstructed by the present.

The truth of memory . . . lies in the story, not as it happened but as it lives on and unfolds in collective memory. . . . [We] are the stories that we are able to tell about ourselves.

History turns into myth as soon as it is remembered, narrated, and used, that is, woven into the fabric of the present.

Jan Assmann, *Moses, the Egyptian*

The more I live in their territory, the more I see and hear them in my mind's ear and eye. Standing exactly where the shaman stood to begin the painting and sitting on the rock where the women prepared the gatherings of the day, I hear conversations and stories. I imagine the women watching their children as they worked, and I imagine the hope and intensity of the men for whom a squirrel would be a blessing.

November 25, 2005 Friday

I skipped yesterday—here, not in life. On Wednesday night I lighted candles in every window and on the steps and turned the porch light off, for effect—though, in the darkness, Tom almost missed the turn that says "Judge Roy Bean," not "Langtry." I was watching the lights of trucks and cars come across the top of the hill, and finally one turned in—Hector, Montana, and Tom. They all came into my house and got oriented. Tom remarked that wild animals get to go wherever they want to, but domesticated animals have to go where they are taken. Hector could have been having Thanksgiving in a Brooklyn apartment, his original home, but instead was in Langtry, Texas.

Thursday I got up and walked up to the church to watch the beautiful sunrise—all pink and gold and gray. I saw a bird, maybe a small roadrunner, but it was standing up too straight as it strutted away. Maybe a quail. I had decided to take Thanksgiving off guilt-free and yet was very aware of following Tom's rhythms more than my own. Had a late breakfast and I read aloud what I had written—more than I expected. I cannot decide if it is any good, but it is my own voice.

Around noon we drove over to Jack and Wilmuth's house and were surprised to find them around the dining table. It had not occurred to me that some folks actually eat Thanksgiving dinner at noon! Jack said to come back at 2 p.m. and we would go into the canyon. I showed Tom the canyons around the old house and we saw one feral hog trotting about. (I have heard they have been around here only about eight years.) Then we came home and had salad—my red beans were slow cooking.

Later Jack took us down to Eagle Nest Canyon. The road to the river is rough and steep, and down river a bit it curves back into the canyon. Jack showed us where Guy, his dad, drove his tractor off the road and tumbled pretty far down the hill—until the tractor tires landed on two rocks and luckily he fell between them! Before the Rio Grande was dammed to make Lake Amistad, the river was high enough for waterskiing. Then the river silted up and the water level became what it is now.

In the middle of the canyon is a dry basin that used to be a lovely spring. Guy first used an electric pump to bring its water to the top of the cliff. After the pump washed away in the 1954 flood spawned by a hurricane, Guy told Jack that he was going to build a windmill. When Jack pointed out that there was not enough wind down in the canyon, Guy said, "Hell, I'm going to put in on top." "How are you going to do that?" "Watch and I'll show you." And he did it with cables and pulleys that went down 150 feet off the bluff to a pump that pulled on the down stroke.

Guy would listen to the weather report every night, and, if a freeze was expected, he would go to the bottom of the canyon—a very steep trail, almost straight down—to drain the pipe. Finally, he got tired of doing that and figured out how to disconnect the pipe from the top. I said it sounds as if he was the kind of man who could figure out anything—and Jack said, "Yes, he could even take a watch apart and put it back together."

Jack showed us a huge boulder that had washed far downstream during the flood. It had rained hard all night and the water came up very high in the canyon. It's hard to imagine a boulder as big as a house floating!

We climbed up into a huge shelter—like an amphitheater—a perfect shape with high, curved ceiling and a floor of ten to fifteen feet of burned rock and ashes with all kinds of things mixed in—quid (remains of chewed lechuguilla), tools, and much else. Jack has not dug there at all, but in the 1930s, Witte Museum people dug a trench that is still there. Jack thinks future archaeologists will probably be as aghast at current methods as we are at earlier ones.

People keep coming up with new ways to study these early people. A woman was here a few months ago studying sound in shelters that were used for habitation. Someone else wanted Jack to send them some dirt to look for something—can't remember what. Anyway he gets contacted all the time by scholars studying flora, fauna, and people unique to this very place.

In this shelter, there were a lot of rock paintings, but most of these have been erased one way or another. I studied the pictures in the Kirkland/Newcomb *The Rock Art of Texas Indians* to see more clearly the images that I could now just barely make out on site: a wonderful anthropomorphic figure and more of those boxes that I like so much.

We went into a smaller shelter on the other side of the canyon—perhaps it was a winter shelter. It was hot and the afternoon sun has faded the painted images. One big smooth boulder is covered with grinding holes. I sat up there and tried to visualize other women sitting here ages ago. I could almost hear the murmuring talk. Some of the grinding holes in the canyon floor are an arm's length deep. Jack said they cooked in them or fermented things—I don't know what. It is hard to realize they had only baskets or animal skins for containers—no pottery.

When we drove out of the canyon, we stopped at the river. The shore is muddy and the water brown, though they said it was clearing up. We saw one scurrying armadillo.

Back at the Skiles' house we had tea and cookies and then came on home to cook rack-of-lamb in the clay pot for our Thanksgiving dinner. It was truly, incredibly, and wonderfully delicious. (I tried not to think about the precious lambs on the ranch.)

It is 9 a.m. Friday. The animals are resting, and Tom is drinking coffee and reading. I am still trying to hold on to the "what is supposed to happen will happen" concept.

I get really blue at night. Tom says that is when he feels good—it is in the morning that he gets discouraged. I cannot imagine that, but I guess it illustrates the attraction of opposites. For me, mornings are wonderful. After dark, I feel more relaxed in the house with other people (and animals) here. I love having the window shades open even though I cannot see anything except lights of trucks and trains.

Almost There

Approaching the end of the trail,
straining for arrival,
I climb toward an overhang
shelter on the steep cliffs
above the Devils River with its
ancient painting of the
Panther with the Curled Tail.
I am the latest among those who
for ten thousand years, give or take,
have sought shelter here.

Finally I enter the shade of the rock
and the panther looms above me.
To my surprise and disappointment,
I feel no relief.
From this narrow shelf
more paths open.
I did not expect that
nor desire it.
I believed that when I reached this point
I would have something, know something,
be someone.

Paths in the canyon
paths in heart and mind
in imagination and in fact
a long time ago and now
in this place and vistas unlimited
spiral together.
I swoon and lie low.

New paths, rougher, tougher,
bombard me, call me.
I keep reaching out—but
never reaching.

I ought not be surprised
when my destinations are not
endings. After all, I am not all that
familiar with arrivals. Shaped
by wide-open country with
far horizon, I long for
I know not what.

In stories, seekers find their treasures,
return with the boon,
and spend the rest of
their days telling tales of setting out,
retrieval, and return.

Perhaps one day I too
will arrive.
Perhaps one day
I will return with a boon
and stories,
my treasure,
my stories.

Where the Gods Walk

Sacred space—
where the gods walk with
or without human awareness,
or so we hope.
Some say those who name the sacred
create it,
but others say we only discover
what is already there.

Long, long ago, in memory
and longer than that
when animals and humans were one,
before the split, before the fall,
sacred was not found and named.
All was mystery, everything sacred,
alive, listening, speaking—
all messages were crucial.

A sacred place is where I encounter the unknown,
knowing the unknown is not emptiness.
It draws me as it terrifies.
Is my imagination large enough to create it,
to encompass it?
I do not know.
The sacred seems both within me
and surrounding me,
but I am not sure.

I approach a painting on cave wall
never doubting that it was sacred
to those who painted it.
How deep must I go to
cross the threshold?

Hernandez Trail

The sky is overcast, but here in west Texas that does not mean anything. The weather can change to rain a gully-washer or to open up to an unclouded day while you are tightening your bootlaces. I like the light in this grayness. It is not oppressive but soft, as is the moist air on my face, a change from the dry heat we west Texans are so proud of.

For a week I have been tantalized by the promise of hiking the Hernandez Trail. Some friends went on Monday and came back with a good report. Now it is Friday and Elton Pruitt has agreed to take me out there in his new powerful Toyota truck. Like Elton, it can climb rocks you would swear were far too steep and rough for passage. Elton is an archaeologist who has been coming to the lower Pecos for over twenty years.

After college, he joined with other archaeologists to do a survey of these canyons before the dam was finished across the Rio Grande near Del Rio and the new Lake Amistad filled up. Generally, his natural talents and interests go to exploration and he mostly leaves the theories to others. Elton loves this country; it is in his blood. And he is a self-proclaimed mountain goat. He sees paths where I see only boulders. Though he has been to this site many times, he acts as if there is little he had rather do than climb down this rock wall.

We drive down a series of natural rock shelves—no road. I began early on asking if we should not walk from here—or from the next drop. I am afraid that Elton may be too proud of his truck's rock-climbing abilities, too eager to show me what this baby can do. But he knows just where to stop. We gather our binoculars, water, and walking sticks and head down the path.

The start of a trail both thrills and scares me. I am eager to see what is around the next bend, yet I am not positive my legs and my balance are up to it. I encourage myself with stories of others who have gone before. Yesterday I met a woman who did this trail with a leg brace, though now Elton tells me her going was ill-advised at best. He is a genial guide but has no desire to carry anyone back up the trail.

Here at the top of this trail the rocks appear to be scraped. Elton tells me that someone had worked on the trail with his Bobcat bulldozer. Before that, the trail had not been usable in a long time. The angle of the hill makes me wonder how on earth anyone could use that dozer here, but then I realize that this dozer and Elton's truck are more than tools for these men. There is definitely cowboy energy at work—or at play. Though the dozer had erased clues to the exact location of the original trail's start, lower down you know it is the old trail because it is the only one possible at this place on the river.

This trail goes down a steep cut created over thousands of years by the Pecos River. But the side we are on is nothing like the sheer cliff of red stone on the other side of the river. There the vertical wall is broken only by a few small indentions just large enough to offer a hawk a river-watching spot. As we descend, we hear a hawk before we see it swooping up the river in front of us. The sight of this raptor is inspiring, reminding me of Gerard Manley Hopkins's description of a falcon: "My heart in hiding / Stirred for a bird,—the achieve of; the mastery of the thing!"

Unlike passing glimpses of hawks in trees along the highway, here I have no doubt that I am an outsider in this hawk's native land. The hawk in flight, its shadow on the cliff, the clouds moving across sky, and the flow of the Pecos are so integral to each other and so powerful that I almost lose my balance—on the trail and in my mind. I am disoriented in both body and spirit. Although I don't actually feel the earth turning on its axis or moving around the sun, I imagine that is a natural extension of what I feel. All move together.

We know this trail was used in the 1800s for crossing the Pecos, but now it is hard to see exactly where it comes out on the west side of the river. It is a puzzle to study the rock falls and brush lines for clues to where earlier folks found their way up. We cannot reach the river because it now covers the tops of the salt cedar trees which grow on a small strip of land on this side of the river (the vega). From the 1920s until recently, local folks gathered here for picnics. Elton points out wires used to lower boats to the river.

As the path gets narrower and steeper, Elton taps along with his hiking stick to warn critters that we are coming. And, sure enough, one hears him—a truly giant skunk appears on the narrow trail ahead of us. At first I am positive we are going to have to go back, because there will be no going sideways for either the skunk or us. The skunk suddenly slips through an opening on the rocks not immediately visible to us and we walk on by. The skunk belongs here in a way I do not—but would like to.

About half-way down the cliff, we take an uphill fork in the trail and climb up to our destination—a ledge where low on the wall there is a red drawing, a single human-like figure, about eighteen inches high. It is camouflaged in the shadows and in the natural shadings of the hillside. We look closely but do not see any other painted images.

The narrow ledge widens just a bit at the opening to a low cave, which is too wet and too small to lure me in, although I am curious to know if there is more rock art inside. Near the cave is a huge boulder about six feet high with many grinding holes in it. As I touch the smooth sides of these stone cups, I know that the people who came here to paint and to grind found a cool place to work and, like us, to sit in the shade, feel the breeze, and watch the hawks and their companion reflections on the river.

11

On the Move

[Entering today's world, our ancient ancestors would] miss the
close ties of kinship, the intimacy of small-community life, the shared
responsibilities of hunting, gathering, and defense, the working
interactions with nature, the rites and rituals, the myths and legends
of heroes, gods, and goddesses, and the magical sense of living in an
animated world.

Anthony Stevens, *The Two Million-Year-Old Self*

We do not know the language of the early people of the lower Pecos, but we can imagine ways they spoke of the land. Today the silence of absent canyon voices is broken only by wind, by birds' wing and call, by deer, turkey, javelina, and feral hogs foraging in the grasses on the canyon floor. Yet it is easy to conjure the sounds of people busy in the canyon, families talking about children, elders, and ancestors, about food and shelter, about the sun, the moon, and the seasons, about sacred rituals and spirits felt even if unseen.

November 29, 2005 Tuesday

I have not written since Friday. It is surprising that I got any writing done while Tom was here. He left Sunday afternoon. I slept a long time last night. It was so cold I didn't want to get up and went back to sleep. It is now 10:40 a.m. I am going to work on the Primitive chapter today.

As the sun came up, I thought of the early families watching the sky and pondering the movement of the sun and stars and planets and moon. When I watch the sun come up from very first light—now about 6:20 a.m.—until the very tip appears about 7:18 a.m., I can almost feel how fast this planet is rotating and realize we are moving on an axis and whizzing around the sun at the same time. But mostly, of course, I think I am still and the sky is moving.

Ponder at the Gate

I

Ranch roads in west Texas are often
long and seldom smooth.
You need heavy-duty tires,
four-wheel drive, high clearance,
and a good map.
A wrong turn can leave you lost,
stuck, or stranded,
or worse.

Ranch gates present obstacles
and opportunity.
Passing through may lead to
disaster or adventure.
If you are not careful,
if you don't watch out,
something might be let out, or in.

A ranch gate may have many locks.
You have to know
which combination goes with which lock
and you must never double-lock.
A rancher does not like to drive slow and far
down the almost impassible rocky road
to be locked out.
But, with luck, the lock clicks,
the gate swings open
and the pickup bumps on through.

II

Passage has been made and all is changed
even here where it appears nothing has changed
ever.
Threshold or cattle guard, a departure, an arrival,
there, here,
close but all the difference.

A choice—go on or turn back.
Down the road beyond the gate,
how far can you see?
How much can you know for sure?

III

Even a solid rock might be a threshold,
or so they tell me.
The pied piper sounds the note,
the mountain opens
and then closes forever.
An ancient mark painted on a wall,
a message to the gods passed on through
to the other side or brought
over here from over there.

The wall—barrier and threshold—
to whatever your soul can imagine.
Images of creatures not seen in this world
float to the surface to be held there by painters
who are watching for them, prepared.

Visions arrive like answers
on a magic ball
and if you are ready,
if you are of the right mind and heart,
perhaps you see them.
How many appear never to pass through?

IV

Ranch gate, rock wall—
places of choice, of courage.
When the song of the piper or the call
of the sirens voids choice altogether
you must go.
No matter, no regard.

But at some doors, a decision must be made.
Perhaps courage means standing still or turning back,
perhaps choosing means stepping forward
boldly, fearfully, fast, or slow.
It doesn't really matter how,
only if.

Standing at the door, the opening,
passageway, gate, threshold—
naming and naming to delay the moment—
wondering, pondering,
will crossing put me in or out?

Both, of course,
always both,
gain and loss either way
and always less choice—
more piper, more siren.
The only thing you really have
to worry about is getting stuck
on the cattle guard.

Sight Unseen:
Painted Rock Shelter

Heading for Painted Rock Shelter, we leave Highway 90 just east of the Pecos River and go through the first of a series of gates that mark boundaries between several ranches, all belonging to Zuberbueler cousins. Swiss immigrants, the first Zuberbuelers had been ranchers in the northern Mexico state of Chihuahua for thirteen years before moving across the Rio Grande to Texas. In the early 1900s, John Zuberbueler and his son Emil bought this land between the Pecos and the Rio Grande, sight unseen.

They were confident that this ranch, bordered by three rivers (the Pecos, the Devils, and the Rio Grande), would be excellent for raising cattle. When Emil arrived with the first load of steers, he discovered what the selling agent had not revealed—the land was on the rivers all right, but steep cliffs made the water inaccessible to the livestock. Nevertheless, they stayed. Emil acquired two more sections by homesteading for the three years necessary to claim ownership. Emil and his wife, Louisa, built a house beside a stream and eventually owned a spread of over three thousand acres. When they died, their six children divided this large ranch.

On this day in April of 2003, our group's destination is the Harrington Ranch owned by Jack and Missy Harrington. Missy is the granddaughter of Emil and the daughter of Eline "Tootsie" Zuberbueler King, Emil and Louisa's daughter. Missy, Jack, and archaeologists Dr. Carolyn Boyd and Elton Pruitt are leading us to an important rock art site used for thousands of years by hunter-gatherer people here on the eastern edge of the Chihuahuan desert.

Six of us have come together for a week at Shumla School, which Boyd and her husband, archeobotanist Dr. Phil Dering, founded with the Harringtons and Pruitt (who first came to this area in 1970 to survey shelters that were soon to be inundated by Lake Amistad on the Rio Grande). Named for a nearby railway stop, Shumla's goals are to educate people of all ages about the lifeways of the archaic peoples who inhabited this area for over 10,000 years and whose legacy is some of the most outstanding and well-preserved rock art in the world and to study and record this rock art.

The rock art of the lower Pecos, as it is called, is not well known even among Texans. Most is on private ranches whose owners do not readily welcome visitors. Although the value of these sites has become more recognized in the past few decades, until recently serious study has been limited. Missy and her mother both grew up familiar with mysterious drawings on the canyon walls of their ranch but say they never gave it much thought until the day Elton and others came and asked permission to record it. Until then, it had just seemed a natural part of a south Texas ranch since rock art was everywhere around here.

Now on this narrow two-rutted ranch road, we wind and twist, cross streambeds (wet and dry), and circle the desert hills. The only sounds are bird songs and the screech of cactus etching the paint on our passing pickups. With our binoculars we can see tall chimneys across the canyon—all that is left of the house Emil and Louisa built. A huge vulture perches atop one chimney, a perfect spot for spying rats, snakes and rabbits— pretty much anything that moves (or has ever moved). Even from this distance, the vulture's huge, powerful wings startle us as it takes off on a mission.

Crossing several ranches means passing through gates. Some do not require the normal gate ritual of disembarking, unlocking, opening, driving through, closing, locking, getting back aboard, because they are "bump gates." You touch the gate with your bumper ("kiss it") and then you press firmly on the accelerator, knock the gate open, and fly through before it slams back into you. Each successful passage is a victory and shows that this driver knows this place and merits passage.

As the road narrows between a canyon and a hillside, we learn that the hill is covered with fossils from when the shallow sea that covered most of Texas receded between 100 and 65 million years ago. I climb up the hill to see them, but I only find rocks. Soon, however, I realize that every rock is actually a shell or a cluster of shells. Many of the shell fossils look like curved rams' horns, appropriate for this country now used more for sheep than cattle.

Out here in this dusty land under the blazing sun in a cloudless blue sky, I quickly learn that just because something is visible does not mean I can see it. Awareness of this fact, however, does not help that much. I see when someone points and names. Snakes and lizards, rabbits and birds are camouflaged and blend into rocky ground, rough bark of shrubs, and shadows. I ponder the vision of the early hunter-gatherers, whom I have come to study for my dissertation in mythology. But I recognize my relation to them in Ernest Becker's praise of another hunting group: "The Australian aborigine had a richness of perception, a refinement of analysis, a wisdom of his world, that would make a Ph.D. anthropologist seem like an imbecile in that setting."

Walking down the hill toward the canyon, we see grey rock scattered about but don't think much of it until Elton explains that we are looking at burned rock middens, the stone mounds of ancient ovens utilized by people who long ago cooked sotol or lecheguilla plants right here. This method of cooking has been dated to at least ten thousand years ago. Now we notice that the ancient fires have cracked all the rocks into same size and shapes. Pointing out that the rocks of each midden have been thrown out in the same direction, Elton explains that the prevailing wind here is from the southwest— is now and always has been—so, to avoid the smoke, they (and we) would logically open the fire with the wind behind us. For a moment, time condenses and I see early nomads tossing still-warm stones to the places they lie yet. This is the first of many times I sense their presence. As the old Zuberbueler homestead had connected us to this early rancher, the grandfather of our host Missy Harrington, so these burned stones connect us to the first people on this land. With these middens, they left their mark on the land where I now join them. I pick up a rock that was in another's hand thousands of years ago. It does not feel mysterious or impossible; it feels natural. Its weight and texture in my hand instills a strong yearning, but I know not what I seek or what longing this place and these people arouse.

At noon, we eat our picnic lunches, sitting with our backs to the wind in the thin shade of small bushes. Looking at the rocky hill, I have a moment of disorientation. I struggle to remember where I am in time and in space. The land looked just like this thousands of years ago, though at times this area was drier or grassier and inhabited by buffalo. Long before buffalo, now-extinct mammals grazed here— mammoths, camels, saber-toothed tigers, and long before that there were dinosaurs. With the passage of so much time, with wind and sun as constants, I imagine looking down on this scene from the

moon and realize the nature of my confusion. With time spans
and distances too vast to comprehend, human-made divisions seem
inconsequential, ridiculous even.

A few clouds give us intermittent relief from the intense Texas
sun. We have always called it the "Texas sun" as if it was uniquely
ours, special, or especially hotter. But we are only a half-mile from the
Rio Grande, and the political boundaries between Texas and Mexico,
established in 1842, lose reality. In some ways, they have never been
much more than lines on maps. Although the rivers have always
created their own boundaries, the entire United States-Mexican
border has been a country of its own. The river has always had
crossing places and before the dam was built here, the Rio Grande
was often only a trickle. When Missy's grandfather moved his cattle
from Mexico, he built a one-lane bridge for walking them across.
Now the border looms big in the story of who and where we are. I
look south to see the mountains in Mexico—a distant and foreign
land in some stories, near and familiar in others. I can't keep it all
straight.

Indigenous blood runs on both sides of the Rio Grande—in the
borderlands. Perhaps these foragers from four thousand years ago are
ancestors of the people who live in the borderlands of the southwest
United States, the Papago, the Paiutes, or of those in the northernmost
part of Mexico, the Tarahumara, the Yaquis, or the Huichols, who
now live farther south. No one knows for sure what became of
the people who left their mark in the lower Pecos region, but the
best guess is that they gradually joined with other groups, many of
whom had begun cultivation of small fields long before these hunters
joined them. That is the best guess, but what feels truer is that they
disappeared in the "dim mists of time"—actually and mythically.

After lunch we head down to see the rock art by the creek. The
rocky path is not steep, but it is treacherous. Each time my mind
wanders, I slip. (I slip a lot.) We descend gradually through shrubs
and cacti, all bearing thorns and definitely unsuitable to grab for
balance. I see something move—a tarantula—a sight that has always
terrified west Texas kids like me. We believed these scary-looking
creatures could march down the street to find you and kill you. Out
here, this huge spider with its black furry legs is at home in what to

me is a surreal and almost hostile landscape. We part with this one on good terms.

Half-way down the hill, we enter the shell of an old one-room structure called the Millman house. The only information about it is derived from rumor. It might have been a hide-a-way for smugglers or for lawmen in their pursuit. We duck under the weathered wooden lintel into the skeleton of the house. The rock work is sturdy. Each of the large stones was brought from several miles away and placed to fit with adjacent stones to withstand over one-hundred years of wind, rain, and "Indian depredations." On one stone is carefully etched "John Greenfield."

Missy and Carolyn earlier took up the challenge of finding out who he was. They learned that there was a person named Greenfield in a nearby town. When they called her, she was amazed and thrilled to know that her ancestor had made his mark on stone out in this wilderness. She came to see it with her own eyes, touch it with her own hands. Right here had stood the grandfather she had barely known.

Signaling to any rattlesnake whose natural habitat this surely must be, I tap with my hiking stick as I leave this small fort-like house and wonder how much longer it will endure. I sadly envision the day the rest of the stones must inevitably fall among the ones already scattered about.

Behind the house, I climb over small boulders to reach a much more ancient site of human activity. At the bottom of the hill, a small stream sweeps along the base of an overhang called "Painted Rock Shelter." Today, Carolyn and Elton, who have been here many times before, suddenly stop in their tracks. I know before I am told that something terrible has happened. What they had expected to see is not there.

Ten days ago, a big rain fell in Val Verde County. In this dry and rocky country, a quick big rain is called a "gully-washer" and for good reason. Creeks that normally only trickle can flood instantly when a powerful force of water hurls itself down the arroyos. Many tales begin with someone being told to watch out when hiking down a long-dry riverbed and laughing in the face of such a seemingly absurd warning. These canyons look as if they have never seen rain. But these tales can end with tragedy for those who do not listen. People who live out here are hardy of necessity, not given to fear of nature's harshness, and, when they speak of dangers, the wise heed their words and the unwise soon become wise.

Last week the floods here on this creek unlodged a huge oak tree and washed it through a meander that curved into Painted Cave. The uprooted oak scraped across the wall of the shelter obliterating portions of pictographs that had been there over four thousand years. It now is wedged across the stream just below the shelter.

Carolyn, Elton and the Harringtons are clearly shaken by this irreplaceable loss. Throughout this lower Pecos area, the destruction of rock art is inevitable. The rocks spall—pieces just fall off. The images get covered with algae and dust—the elements take their toll. Natural erosion frustrates efforts to make out whole images from the paint that remains. But the violence of this one rain storm is a shocking reminder of the fragility of the record still available to us in places like this.

The rock art here at Painted Rock Shelter is of particular interest because, of the four primary types of rock art identified by archaeologists in the lower Pecos (grouped by age and style), three are represented here. The oldest, termed Pecos River Style, has been dated from about 4200 to 3000 BP. It is remarkable that these artisans figured out how to make paint that would survive exposure to the elements for over four millennia. Their use of blood and urine as binders makes radio-carbon dating possible. The large, multicolored (red, orange, black, yellow) images are primarily anthropomorphs, (human-like figures), their tools of atlatls (spear-throwers) and spears, animals (deer, felines, canines), and geometric figures. These Pecos River images are so high on the wall that at first I did not even notice them above the more recent style, Red Monochrome, dated to about 1300 BP.

At eye-level, the Red Monochrome images are less stylized and therefore easier to recognize as humans, some with bows and arrows, animals (turkey, turtle, feline, deer), and geometrics. Today their lower parts are dim if discernible at all after the damage of the storm. As we move up the creek bed, Carolyn points out the third type of pictographs found here at Painted Rock Shelter, the Red Linear Style (from about 1100 BP). These are tiny stick figures—humans in group activities. One group appears to be dancing pregnant women. The fourth style, Historic, (c.500 BP to 350 BP) is identified by elements that indicate European contact (churches, horses, cattle, European clothing).

I stand close enough to touch the Painted Rock walls, yet they seem unreachable. From where I stand, the paintings are in my sight but I cannot see them. They cannot be read or otherwise absorbed in my language and culture of analysis, logic and judgment. Still I yearn to cross over, to leave my usual structures of understanding, and to enter the world of the makers of these images. I want to understand the magnetism that pulls me to their world.

We leave the shelter and head back up the hill toward our trucks, sad about the loss of part of this ancient treasure. Though we are little wiser about the lives and thoughts of those who painted here so long ago, we have seen firsthand the potential for destruction of their art by natural forces and by humans and we understand that they may be lost forever.

12

All around the Town

Some people think human beings are the ground where the gods dwell, but I am sure that it is not in us but in the interworld between sacred space and us that the gods finally arise.

Joan Halifax, *Fruitful Darkness*

I go to the canyons of the ancient shelter homes if not to find ancient stories, then to discover or reshape my own. I seek origins. I make a pilgrimage to discover the sacramental nature of landscape, to experience the liminal space of this ancient art, to reawaken the numinous if not as it was in the beginning then as it is now.

November 30, 2005 Wednesday

8:03 a.m.—Warmth (it is a cold fifty-two in the house) and food. I notice everything here more than at home. Eating by myself all the time makes food not so interesting and makes chocolate a necessity.

Nights alone continue to be a problem. I awaken and cannot go back to sleep. The only noise in the house is the hot water heater. Occasionally I can hear the rusty wind chimes that I found on the ground and put back on the sagebrush.

Working back in time—a few catch-up notes: yesterday I worked all day on Chapter 2 and that was sort of fun until I got tired. The part I like best is Jan Assmann's discussion in *Moses the Egyptian* of mnemohistory—the idea that stories rather than historical facts shape lives and cultures.

Eva Ann [Eva Ann Cunningham, Tom's sister] was going to come yesterday, but she decided to come next Tuesday instead. That gives me something to work toward. I am thinking now that I will move home on the 9th. I have to think what my time in this place means to me and why it is so hard to give it up, even though I know I want to be home with Tom. It is easier to work here, and I hope that momentum will keep me going.

Tom and I got more done than usual, though it is amazing how much more energy we have when we are alone than when together. He says it is because together we have all we need for a life.

I can't remember exactly what we did Friday and Saturday. It was Saturday that Tom gave me his pep talk about my project. We went to Jack's museum and then had barbeque sandwiches at Mike's and then went to Pete's. Pete took us all around—even down to his special place on the Rio Grande. He showed us a room he cut out of the cane, his sanctuary. Said he used to come down here just to sit and remember things. He is about to turn eighty-nine and is in remarkable health. Climbs up and down the cliffs without a pause. He told us we should go slowly, that he was fast because he had done it all his life.

I almost stepped on a snake. It was a harmless king snake, but it scared me by its sudden appearance on the trail (or by my sudden noticing). In spite of my vigilance, the two snakes I have seen out here were frighteningly near to me by the time I saw them.

Pete took us to a cave up toward Pump Canyon. Its low ceiling was black from smoke of a million fires. On the floor were grinding holes, but you would have to be very short to use them. Pete said he studies those (man-made? woman-made?) holes and thinks of the people—wonders what they thought about sitting there looking over the river.

Pete also drove us down the old railroad path and up the hill to see the new water works. Told us about many of the early (and late) Langtry settlers. Tom and I both were taken with the one-room studio/residence of Chris Hale, a New York artist who died several years ago but whose place remains just as it was when he lived here painting and sculpting. We looked through the window. His room looks like a dust-covered museum installation.

The postmaster lives in a house Chris owned across the road. It is one of the oldest among the many old houses in Langtry. Seems he came here some time ago to sell fudge by the roadside, then began working at the post office. Tom thinks that looks like the perfect job. The tiny post office is open every morning for residents from ranches near and far to pick up incoming mail, drop off the outgoing, buy stamps and study the wanted posters.

Our busy day wore us out, so we had free time until dusk when we walked over to the old railroad bridge across from the house. Saw a white-tailed deer run over the hill and heard shots nearby. I hope they missed. (It is now mule deer season, which lasts only two weeks.)

We explored a rustic, rusty dump at the bottom of the hill. Around the remains of a burned-out car we found three letters—"R," "E," "R," and hunted for more to complete "RAMBLER," but we didn't find them. Tom said maybe it was ERR—a sign for us. I said, "A sign about my continuing this project?" He said, "No, about your trying to quit!"

On Friday, I showed Tom more of the town, and wewalked down the trail where the railroad tracks used to be. We found the place on the top of Pump Canyon where the old steps went down to Pump Station. Very romantic to me, old pictures show young people climbing down to the swimming hole—men in hats and women in long skirts.

So, today is the last day of November. I came out here on the 10th. Have been back home only five days. Today is the day I had marked to send something to Chris. I will try to finish this second chapter and get it off before Eva Ann comes. I bought lots of bait, so I'll see if Pete wants to go fishing this afternoon—at Jack's, I guess. We'll see. I need to feed my night crawlers.

Later: I did feed my night crawlers—only to discover to my shock and horror that they are chartreuse. I am sure they too would be appalled if they had any self-awareness—as I am assuming they mercifully do not. Then I looked at the box that says that these really catch those fish! Yuk! A fish would only want a green worm if it thought it was a grasshopper and these worms look nothing whatsoever like grasshoppers. Nothing in the natural world is this color except perhaps some parakeets my daddy raised. I always had a pet parakeet when I was little. I would get one now for sentimental reasons, but Hector would kill it immediately.

Reaching Out

Here on this rock one day a long time ago
someone prepared paints—
ground stone, stirred in blood, urine,
and soap from lechuguilla—
created a brush of cactus stalk,
reached toward this place on the wall
and drew a figure
tall with narrow body,
human feet and arms,
and no head at all.
In my mind's eye, the artist
was a woman.

Thousands of years later,
her gestures move me.
Like the pencil drawings of Da Vinci
or the turquoise blue signature of my father,
marks bring their makers very near,
their hands in motion still.

When the woman painted here,
surely she had no imagination of me.
I do not know her mind—perhaps she
thought of eternity, of dangers,
the underworld, the overworld.
Perhaps she had no thought at all.

What I do know is that
today we reach toward
one another,
we touch.

Story on the Wind

There is a woman there (here),
then (now).
She wants to speak.
She calls to me.

At first I cannot hear her.
How do I listen with my eyes,
my imagination, my heart?
How can I open that much?

Come, sit. I am here. Be still.
Time is not as you imagine.
I am your sister, your mother,
your friend.
Our bodies are the same,
our births and birthings,
our deaths and dyings.
We have lived in these canyons
for a long time, and
we are here yet.
Be still. There are truths you do not know.

Once, long ago when I was a small child,
I was playing in this stream.
The water was cool and wonderful,
and rare. We had just celebrated a rain.
I was kicking and flinging the water.
Every drop shone silver and gold.

Then I saw movement in the brush
and stopped to look.
A snake was coming straight toward me
from that low grass there.
I did not move, I could not.

It began to circle me.
When its mouth almost reached its tail,
it moved up and up
and became a bird, curling into the sky—
a beautiful bird like none I had ever seen.

I watched until it disappeared,
and then I hurried up to the shelter
where my mother was grinding acorns.
I told her my story exactly as it happened.

My mother listened and said,
"A snake is a snake, a bird is a bird.
You are dreaming."

I believed what my mother told me—
almost always—
but not this time.
I never doubted and I never forgot—
the water, the snake, the bird,
and the sky.

13

Sunset Gloom, Sunrise Gladness

Each plant or animal has a story of some unique way of living in this world. By tracking their stories down to the finest detail, our own lives may be informed and enriched.

By replenishing the land with our stories, we let the wild voices around us guide the restoration work we do. The stories will outlast us.

Gary Paul Nabhan, *Cultures of Habitat*

My goal is to uncover and recover story by studying the land, reading history, listening to contemporary tales, and imagining life here where lifeways have changed though the land has not. I am trying to learn to see in a new way, deeper, out of the box canyon of my culture by reading the signs that emerge from the experience of being here.

December 1, 2005 Thursday

It seems momentous to have this day—a new month and a full one. Last night I wanted to go home. It was my worst night of thinking I am crazy to be here. I had a bacon-and-eggs comfort dinner and improved a bit. I completely unapologetically (to myself) went to bed at 8:30 p.m. and finished my McGarr murder mystery.

After working all yesterday on the Primitive chapter, I went to get Pete to go fishing. He said it was too late, but we drove on down to the Skiles' place on the river and determined that you can't fish there—not enough shore. Pete said Jack is going to help him put his boat in the river, which might be illegal since this part of the river is actually a national park with "restricted access." But Pete probably would not have any trouble with the law. Besides his being a fixture west of the Pecos, both his sons were high up in the Border Patrol.

I am aware of how soon I am closing up here and going home. Once this is over, I will not come back, or not much probably, and I need to feel I'm down the road on my project.

Tonight was supposed to be "First Thursday Meet and Greet" at the Vashti Skiles Community Center with pot luck supper and business meetings, but some of the board members could not come, so they called it off. I was actually disappointed. I had figured I could take cheese and crackers and share in the folks' excitement about their new self-maintained water system, which is supposed to be completely operational by the end of the week.

Every morning I have watched the sun come up a tiny bit later—7:21 a.m. today. Clear sky, beautiful shades of soft gold/yellow/cream. Watching the first rays hit the top of the hills in Mexico, I think of Tom and me in Kenya at the Lewa Wildlife Conservancy—jumping out of our mosquito-netted bed and hurrying outside to see the sun hit the side of Mt. Kenya—always an anticipated thrill with the possibility of a rhino walking along the ridge across the way.

Yesterday I saw my animals: an armadillo and young hogs—one tiny and really cute (I hope the dead one by the road was not their mother) and a baby deer. The fawn stood not far from Guy's old tractor down by the river and watched us a long time—fearless—until its mother called. It looked exactly like Bambi—exactly.

Tuesday the only animal I saw was a possum on the road. I always drive the back road home from my nightly telephone calls just for the chance to spot a critter.

The artist, Chris Hale, has a brother. We need to find him. Had I rather buy a place here or in Comstock? My first inclination is here, but I think Comstock might be a better plan—considering they are both bad plans.

Jack came to fix my toilet. I didn't tell him that the carport (so-called) almost blew over in the windstorm. I threw some rocks on the roof to hold it down. Pebbles, really, but they kept it from rattling so much.

It is 7:50 a.m. Now I'm going to try to re-read Chapter One and think about why I am here—or anywhere.

Promised Land

[One's] heart seeks to return to a mythical source, a place of "origin," the "home" where the ancestors came from, the mountain where the ancient fathers were in direct communication with heaven, the place of the creation of the world, paradise itself, with its sacred tree of life.

Thomas Merton, *Mystics and Zen Masters*

For thousands of years, ten thousand
that we know of, humans have walked,
stalked, searched, and read this land
of the lower Pecos,
this sacramental landscape,
reminding me of what the earliest
knew from the beginning—
here the gods abide.

Foragers of the lower Pecos were not
seeking meditation but meat,
but they *were* searching,
and in a world of no separation
between sacred and profane,
meat, seeds, roots—
whatever the land provided for nourishment—
was holy, a gift from the gods.

East meets west here
where the passage of searchers forms its history—
Native American hunters and gatherers,
European explorers, settlers up from Mexico and
across from Europe and Asia,
cattlemen and sheepherders,
railroad planners, builders, riders—
a Whitmanesque litany of folks stopping here,
few staying long.

Moving and seeking
lie deep in our souls.
All live the myth of
the eternal return,
ever searching for home,
for Eden.

Seeking not settling,
continually moving toward,
continually moving away,
and gradually accepting
the hard truth:
Eternal return and eternal exodus
are one,
never ceasing, always sacred.

Out of the Shadows

It floated to the surface
shadowy
then suddenly clear.

It had taken the bait on
the dropline nailed to the
sheer rock wall on
the Mexican side of
the Rio Grande.

At first the line came
up easy, loose:
"Check the bait and let it back down—
there's no fish here,"
Pete directed.

As I got ten, twelve, fifteen
feet down the line, tension grew,
probably just the bait, I thought,
huge bait: an eight-inch writhing
channel cat.

Then I saw it floating up
out of the shadows,
the wide, open, whiskered mouth
of the twenty-eight pound
yellow catfish.
I screamed, "Oh my gosh! oh my gosh!"
Grabbing for the line, Pete shouted,
"Don't let go, don't pull,
you have to play it!"

Play this monster?

I had been pulling slowly
and watching about a foot below
the surface where the line disappeared
into the green-brown water
when the mouth rose up
as if in a dream,
ephemeral, inactual,
impossible—
mouth and a strong
whoosh of tail,
a portmanteau creature
a frog-whale, a fish-horse,
a purse-snake.

I jumped up screaming,
almost tipping the boat and
I knew Pete would think
"typical girl-sees-mouse"
but this monster was
no mouse.

He tells the story:
"I knew I had to get
to the front of the boat
fast. I had to let that
line out just right,
let it wear itself out,
and show her how to put the net
up under its tail, just right,
just like that. Bring 'er up!"

Hauling in that fish was thrilling.
I touched its huge yellow-green body
thanking it for sacrificing itself
that I might have supper.

But it was not dead yet.
In fact, it lived far too long after that,
survived the trip back to the cane-hidden
landing, survived being tumped into the tow
sack, survived being hauled up the
hill, survived being dropped
when I could no longer
hold on, even survived
"instant death" promised by the
wire inserted into its skull.

Finally, mercifully, it lay still.
Together we hung it on the tree
with a rope threaded through
its lower lip.
Together Pete and I skinned, gutted,
filleted, fried,
and feasted on
this giant creature from
the depths of the Rio Grande,
so powerful underwater,
its ending beginning
when it fought and floated
out of the shadows.

14

Last Week in Langtry
(or So I Thought)

In Aboriginal belief, an unsung land is a dead land: since, if the songs are forgotten, the land itself will die. To allow that to happen was the worst of all possible crimes.

Bruce Chatwin, *The Songlines*

A man who was born in this country almost nine decades ago took me in his pickup down the rocky switch-back tracks to the Rio Grande and then in his boat down the meandering river. He had a story for each canyon and creek, each cave and crevasse. He pointed with nostalgia to his old fishing and hunting camps. "Over there is the cave where a woman died." "Below that overhang was once a rock art mural." "That eagles' nest has been on that ledge for over one hundred years." "The railroad men camped there." Every twist and turn holds a story that will be lost forever if not remembered and told soon.

December 4, 2005 Sunday

Tonight I am lonesome again. (I'm sounding like an old Elvis or Hank Williams song!) I lighted candles and watched out the window. Being here has been a unique time in my life. I am both eager to get home and sad to leave. Tomorrow night will be my last one alone and that is fine and also good.

Today my animals were a dozen turkeys at Pump Canyon and two deer on the road. I went over to the canyon to call Tom and I think the Border Patrol followed me home. The official vehicle passed by the house going very slowly, creepy and police-state-ish.

It is 8:46 p.m. and if I make it to 9 that will be great! I think I'll read my murder mystery (Nevada Barr).

December 5, 2005 Monday

    I dreamed I was going to graduate school at the University of Texas and had the room of J. Frank Dobie [Texas folklorist].

    I was awake from 2:30 a.m. to 4 a.m. and, for a moment, I felt good about my project. Even in the nighttime! I'm not sure why or even what I thought, but it had to do with the stirring of the spirits— my being here is good or good enough.

December 7, 2005 Wednesday

Once again my sleep was fitful. I was glad when 5 a.m. arrived and I could bring my books in on my bed. (Getting up before 5 just seems just plain wrong to me!) I worked on my project all day yesterday until Eva Ann rolled in right at sunset, our most beautiful one—very pink.

It is a good time for company, because I have sort of vaguely finished Chapters 2 and 3. I want to enjoy the feeling of accomplishment, yet they are in no way ready to send to Chris.

I think I know how to proceed. I honestly feel that even if I get tired and frustrated, I won't get depressed! Ha! *Quelle* claim! But I really believe the "I can't do this" phase has passed. We shall see.

I have changed. At first I walked and explored a lot. This last week I worked more. No walk to the sunrise. It was colder last week and my focus was work.

We leave Friday. In the meantime I want to enjoy everything about being in Langtry. My time alone is over and that's as it should be. I will always look back on this month as very special.

December 8, 2005 Thursday

I went over to Jack and Wilmuth's to ask if I might rent this place for a couple more months. I wasn't sure I wanted to, but when they said okay, I returned to *my* house feeling exuberant. A hawk was flying right over the house. It was the only one I've seen around here. When it landed on the big tower next door, I thought: "Yes! Another sign!"

I love the canyons, sunrises and sunsets, the rocks and the artifacts, the possibility of seeing animals. When I remember this place and time, I'll remember the people and hunting for things, making mandalas, sitting at Pump Canyon, being outside all the time, and writing, of course!

I wish I could have deeper awareness of the moment. Perhaps I can develop it—I have tried here. I want to be thoroughly present today and tomorrow.

December 9, 2005 Friday

Our electricity went off about 8 p.m. It was a bitter cold night.
I am glad we have a gas stove so we can still have coffee. Jack and
Wilmuth bundled up and brought us flashlights. We had candles, but
Eva Ann and I decided to put on lots of clothes (even our caps!) and
go to bed.

I awoke in time to see the sun come up in a clear sky, and then I
got back into bed to wait for electricity and coffee. The thermometer
says it is twenty-two! Jack will be out breaking ice in the tanks for the
sheep. (Yesterday, we helped him round up a sheep that was on the
highway. We saw it and called Jack and Wilmuth on the cell phone:
"Loose sheep at east gate!" I felt sort of like the Border Patrol.)

Eva Ann and I will leave later this afternoon—home for
Christmas and then who knows what?

Going to the River

I had to stay in Langtry
where mornings were glorious
doors and windows wide open
coffee, music and meditations,

where evenings were journeys to
depression and confusion—
in the canyons the sun left early
chill settled in
cold to the bones
loneliness and longing.

I remember these feelings from childhood—
afternoons spent tromping alone
in Mr. Creighton's pasture
exhilarated and scared at the same time,

after supper, listening to my mother's
stories of life at the Costello ranch on the Brazos.
(At every funeral we sang, "Shall We Gather
at the River?" always knowing it was the
Brazos where we would gather.)

Listening to Bible stories at the First Baptist Church:
Zacchaeus, you come down,
Son, you *can* come home again,
Joseph, you look beautiful in that coat.

These stories gave me comfort. They also
created longing that goes on forever,
even here in Langtry,
especially here in Langtry.

Crossing Signs

The Serengeti Plain does not recognize
the border between Kenya and Tanzania,
and why should it?
In 1886, Europeans drew that line, but
wildebeests with cheetahs in
lightning pursuit do not heed the sign
with *Serengeti* on one side
and *Masai Mara* on the other.

Though many in Nairobi and Dar es Salaam
hold the line important, to die for,
the Masai are not concerned—after all,
cattle and their land were given them by God.
Long before the English and Germans arrived
to help them out, Bantus and Kikuyu had their
own ways of marking their homelands.

When I look at the sunrise here in Langtry,
I remember sunrise on Kilimanjaro
and the morning's first rays striking
the top of Mount Kenya.
It has been a long time since those African mornings,
yet the memory moves me still.

Here our border is also marked by a sign,
Rio Grande on one side, *Rio Bravo del Norte* on the other,
but deer do not obey *No Crossing*
nor do the mountain lions stalking them.
This border has been drawn and redrawn by folks
in Mexico City and Washington, D. C.
where the state of Chihuahua and the state of Texas
are worlds apart if you are thinking about sovereignty.

And it is hard not to, with green and white
Border Patrol trucks around every corner, slowly
moving along fence lines, searching for
footprints in the freshly-smoothed dirt.

For hunter-gatherers roaming here
not so long ago, boundaries were rivers and
canyons where certain plants grew
and certain creatures lived.
I am beginning to see as they saw,
and it makes all the difference.

Beyond Intention

To see—that is to discover—is not an act of interpretation, . . .
rather, it is an act of surrender.

—Gretel Ehrlich, "Landscape"

At first glance, the canyons of Langtry
did not scare me. I figured if I read enough
books, hiked enough trails, I would know their
stories, have them well in hand.

But alone in the desert I soon
discovered that here in the land of shamans
I walk dangerous ground,
a thin place between worlds
and particularly permeable.

On the canyon's edge in this wide
open desert, I regard myself
from deep space and
in my very bones feel
my finitude and creatureliness.

In limitless sky and horizonless space,
on the edge of this overhanging rock,
(a perfect shelter for desert rattlers),
I knock stones to the chasm floor.
I must pay attention—
one misstep and I am lost.

By the vastness or by a small
movement under the cactus,
I am overwhelmed.
Without choice, beyond intention,
I surrender.

15

From Big Spring to Langtry

It is not life and death in that sense that I mean, but in the sense of Hamlet's "To be or not to be," which does not mean either to die or to live a few years longer, but to find an answer to the ultimate question of the meaning of life. . . . This is not life in the sense of survival but life in the sense of finding the precious jewel, something that carries ultimate concern.

Paul Tillich

The work came to be not so much about the foraging of the hunter-gatherers but instead about my own foraging—hunting and gathering for survival, my own survival. By *survival*, I do not mean not dying, but living through an experience during most of which I felt I could neither push forward nor turn back—nor just stand still. Finally I was forced to acknowledge that I was digging not into archaic history but, in reality, digging into myself. My work came out of a primal yearning for something unknown yet essential and integral to my personal journey.

Origins

The start of my journey to the lower Pecos country and its rock art shelters can be traced to 1949 when my family moved from Houston to an historic west Texas crossroads, the town of Big Spring. Downtown at the intersection of Gregg Street and Main Street, U. S. Highway 80, the continental route joining San Diego with the outer banks of Georgia, crossed U. S. Highway 87, the intercontinental highway connecting the Gulf of Mexico with Canada. Actually, our precious fountain made Big Spring a crossroads long before the coast-to-coast highway and the Missouri Pacific tracks. To a six-year-old like me, the spring was a mysterious and magical place.

Because the spring was the major water source for miles around, trails spoked to it from all directions. I have heard that ancient routes can still be seen from the air—paths begun perhaps by the earliest mammals grazing here thousands of years before the Spaniards' horses and then were trod upon by the first human travelers to this part of the earth. In more recent times, the Comanche War Trail split off here to take travelers to different parts of Mexico. In 1849, U. S. Army Captain Marcy marked the spring on military maps, indicating that it was a good place to camp on the overland trail to California.

And even greater riches lay at my new home's geographical juncture. Big Spring sits right on the break between the cattle country of the Edwards Plateau to the south and the cotton farms of the Staked Plains, "Llano Estacado," to the north. A few miles west begins the Chihuahuan Desert. To the east Signal Mountain, a rock-capped pyramid-shaped hill, stands alone. They say that, after a raid on a Wells Fargo Payroll Coach, Comanches buried their treasure here, where it remains to this day, protected by rattlesnakes.

I grew up on the western edge of town at the Hitching Post Trailer Park across from the Desert Sands Motel—just west of the Phillips 66 Truck Stop and just east of Webb Air Force Base. Our sky was huge and our vistas wide-open. This is the land that shaped me—hot, windy, dusty, and barren, yet fully provocative.

175

My Shapings

When I was about eight, my folks let me cross the highway to hike around in Mr. Creighton's pasture where I found fossils and bones. Ever alert for rattlesnakes, I worried that I would not have the nerve to cut myself, suck out the poison, and save my own life. Because Webb was a pilot-training base, I occasionally came upon an area strewn with small bits of a crashed plane only to realize that a young man probably died there. Just as this land suffered the harshness of wind sweeping down from the plains, it revealed the reality of death on its very surface.

It was a thrill, however, to wake up every morning to the sight of a distant horizon in every direction. A sign across the street from our house announced: "El Paso 300 Miles." I always imagined heading down that road to discover the exotic world that lay just over the horizon. The west beckoned me, and I yearned to answer the call.

Always and ever in Texas, water and the lack of it are central to life as it is lived. Our family had to make many accommodations to the seven-year drought of 1949-1956. We watched the sky for rain, but dust clouds were all we found. In the fourth grade, I made a large white salt map of Texas with blue rivers the only designated feature—the Nueces, the Colorado, the Guadalupe, the San Felipe, the Navidad, the Frio, the Rio Grande, the Devils, the Pecos, and the Brazos. I loved imagining rivers and *Los Brazos de Dios* (The Arms of God) most of all.

Neither Big Spring's spring nor nearby Moss Creek qualified as a river. My mother, however, grew up on a ranch on the Brazos River in north central Texas. Her stories of life on the Brazos in the early 1900s created a deep longing for that time and place. Her memories filled my imagination. Palo Pinto County and her village of Pickwick held my origin story, my Eden. On the banks of the Brazos, trees draped with wild mustang grapevines gave shade to the Costello and Tennyson family picnics and contrasted diametrically with the sparse vegetation and constant dust storms we suffered in Big Spring during times of drought (most of the time). As a child, I studied Mother's old pictures of dinner-on-the-ground at the Lover's Retreat swimming hole, depicting scenes that heightened my longing. My heart ached for that place and those people and for my mother as she was in these stories. My family-of-origin story begins there long before I was born when all of my grandparents' families immigrated to Palo Pinto County and the Brazos River.

My other origin story was the one in the Bible as taught at the First Baptist Church in Big Spring. Clear in my mind's eye were deserts and waters somewhere far away in the Bible Lands. Abraham and Sarah, Joseph, Moses, King David, Ruth and Naomi, Jesus—who can tell when I first separated them from Maggie and Will, Anna and Don, Mathias and Margaret, Mary Caroline and Beal. All were my ancestors, all traversed great distances looking for better land and water, all suffered vicissitudes. I picture myself a skinny kid steeped in stories standing alone out in Mr. Creighton's pasture studying the ground and the sky, straining to find my place, struggling to get my story straight.

The tradition of story has been a central thread through my life. Progressing from an absorption of childhood books through undergraduate and graduate degrees in literature, I took up storytelling as a career and eventually returned to school to delve more deeply into the mythological stories of the world's cultures. Had I remained true to form, the focus of my dissertation would have been mythic patterns in literature—the world that, heretofore, had been my natural habitat—my primarily *mental* habitat. The long-held attraction to story traditions was such a natural thing that even then I took its source for granted without examination. That changed when I was cast out of the structure—into a world of no text, the rock art of the Lower Pecos. It was the rock art that brought me back to west Texas, but the reason I am here was soon to be discovered in a place far deeper than these canyons.

When first exploring this world during a museum-sponsored trip to Seminole Canyon State Park, I was disturbed by the absence of story. There was nothing to grasp or to be grasped by. After all, no one knows the origins or even the ending of the hunter-gatherers who lived in this area for over nine thousand years, much less the meaning and use of their paintings from four thousand years ago.

So when my husband suggested the lower Pecos and its people and art as a good place to explore mythology and myth-making, my reaction was "Impossible. No one knows who they were." "All the better," he replied. And, it eventually became clear that the trickster, known to be both benefactor and detractor, had snared me once again. Having no other clear options, I resolved to embrace this seemingly impossible task.

Finding My Field

My quest to trick the trickster on this particular subject began comfortably in the familiar world of words—many of them: the writings of archaeologists, historians, art historians, sociologists, and psychologists, to name a few. This pursuit through books gave me the illusion of getting somewhere. By magic and will, I would become an archaeologist with secondary careers in art history and the history of religion. But I found that these writings created their own myths and orientations and disorientations, wove their own mythologies centered not on place but ideas. I was not seeking a place in the abstract. Those written words did not satisfy my interest in the mythic/religious relationship between the most personal and the most universal. My subject is this connection of personal meaning to a sense of place and belonging—finding my place in Big Spring, on the lower Pecos, and in the cosmos.

After one year of reading and taking notes and finding myself boxed inside a mental canyon, I discovered that my inspiration did not spring from the field of archaeology. It directed me instead to a related field, that is, to the "field" itself. I had to go—mind and body, heart and soul—to the canyon lands of the lower Pecos to live on the land with the people there now in order to experience the land of rock art images and to describe my imagination of the people who lived there and painted them. At the same time, I was experiencing an urgency to get my own story straight, to understand the great longing this place stirred in me.

After settling into the house I rented in Langtry, I began the process by writing poems and stories and essays in response to the land and people around me. A trail out of the box canyon opened before my eyes as all my childhood curiosities were awakened: What were the stories of the people? What or how could they see that I could not? How can I imagine their world and what does that teach me about myself? Who am I here? What spirits are astir in this place?

Are These My People, Too?

Pondering stories of Paleoindians led to an exploration of my own origin story, not from *a* beginning but from *the* beginning. On a genealogical chart, I can trace my family back to England and Ireland, to the Norman invaders. From there I vaguely assume a relation with the Romans, Greeks, and somehow to Jesus and the Fertile Crescent and even before that to Adam and Eve. My chronology, obviously, does not have to be *true*, it just needs to work for *me*.

My home on this land was inherited from ancestors who arrived a mere two hundred years ago or so. The foragers who hunted around the confluence of the Rio Grande, the Pecos and the Devils River thousands of years ago arrived by a different route. No one knows exactly how, when, or from whence they came. It is unlikely they are of Irish stock, nor am I Native American. So how can these be my people or I their descendent? I cannot claim them by blood, still I feel that we are somehow related. It is the place itself that creates kinship. Imagining their lives here so long ago opens me to this place, and the place opens me to them.

Myths and sacred stories of the lower Pecos people surely grew out of their experience in this place and are reflected in the mysterious rock art images. Aware that such traditions continue to grow out of lives still lived in this place, I go to the canyons of the ancient shelter homes, if not to find ancient stories, then to discover or reshape my own. I seek origins. I make a pilgrimage to discover the sacramental nature of landscape, to experience the liminal space of this ancient art, to reawaken the numinous if not as it was in the beginning, then as it is now.

Rearview Mirror

After I completed my work in Langtry in 2005, I continued to rent the house from the Skiles month by month. I could not let it go. After I defended my dissertation in 2006, I asked myself what the writing process had been all about. There is no complete answer but my title is clear in one respect. I am now the full-fledged owner of the house.

When the Skiles' offered to sell it to me, I held my breath in fear that they would change their minds. I told my husband I would give up all I owned to buy it. Even though it is unlikely we will ever live there full time, I go there as often as possible to continue digging into the life of Langtry and its canyons.

Recently, I was asked what gives me joy, and the first thing that came to mind was the view out my Langtry front door (as painted by Becky Whitehead on the cover) at the sky, the canyons, the hills of Mexico, the buildings of our town on the river. Questions remain about the mystery of my being there, but I no longer question whether or not I belong.

San Antonio, Texas
August 8, 2014

References and Readings

Abram, David. *The Spell of the Sensuous: Perception and Language in a More-Than-Human World*. New York: Vintage, 1996. 22, 52, 53.

Aqua, Karen. *Ground Zero/Sacred Ground*. http://karenaqua.com/ground_zero.html.

Assmann, Jan. *Moses the Egyptian: The Memory of Egypt in Western Monotheism*. Cambridge: Harvard UP, 1997. 9, 14-15.

Becker, Ernest. *The Birth and Death of Meaning*. New York: The Free Press, 1971. 4.

Bond, D. Stephenson. *Living Myth: Personal Meaning as a Way of Life*. Boston: Shambala, 1993. 16.

Boyd, Carolyn E. *Rock Art of the Lower Pecos*. College Station: Texas A&M UP, 2003.

Brown, Norman O. *Love's Body*. New York: Vintage, 1966. 247.

Buber, Martin. *I and Thou*. 2nd ed. Trans. Ronald G. Smith. New York: Scribner's, 1958.

---. *The Life of the Hasidim*. Trans. Olga Marx. New York: Schocken, 1991.

Bynner, Witter, Trans. *The Way of Life according to Laotzu*. New York: John Day, 1944.

Chatwin, Bruce. *The Songlines*. New York: Penguin, 1988. 52.

Dinesen, Isak. *Out of Africa*. New York: Modern Library, 1983. 4.

Ehrlich, Gretel. "Landscape." *The Legacy of Light*. Ed. Constance Sullivan. New York: Knopf, 1987. 20-22.

Gopnik, Adam. "The Last of the Metrozoids." *The New Yorker*. May 10, 2004.

Halifax, Joan, *Fruitful Darkness: Reconnecting with the Body of the Earth*. HarperSanFrancisco, 1993. 18.

Heschel, Abraham J. *The Prophets.* New York: Perennial, 2001. xxv.

Hillman, James. *Healing Fiction.* Woodstock, CT: Spring, 1983. 23.

Kirkland, Forest, and W. W. Newcomb. *The Rock Art of Texas Indians.* Austin: U of Texas P, 1967.

Krutch, Joseph Wood. *The Desert Year.* New York: Penguin, 1952. 4, 5.

Lopez, Barry. *Crossing Open Ground.* New York: Vintage, 1989. 65.

Merton, Thomas. *The Asian Journal of Thomas Merton.* Ed. Naomi Burton, Brother Patrick Hart, and James Laughlin. New York: New Directions, 1973. 81.

---.*Mystics and Zen Masters.* New York: Delta, 1967. x.

---.*New Seeds of Contemplation.* New York: New Directions, 1961. 1.

Nabhan, Gary Paul. *Cultures of Habitat: On Nature, Culture, and Story.* Washington, D. C.: Counterpoint, 1979. 12.

--- and Mark Klett. *Desert Legends: Re-Storying the Sonoran Borderlands.* New York: Holt, 1994.

Rilke, Rainer Maria. "Duino Elegies." *The Selected Poetry of Rainer Maria Rilke.* Ed. and trans. Stephen Mitchell. New York: Vintage International, 1989. 201.

Schama, Simon. *Landscape and Memory.* New York: Vintage, 1996.

Shafer, Harry J. *Ancient Texans: Rock Art and Lifeways along the Lower Pecos.* Austin: Texas Monthly Press, 1986.

Skiles, Jack. *Judge Roy Bean Country.* Lubbock: Texas Tech UP, 1996.

Stevens, Anthony. *The Two Million-Year-Old Self.* College Station: Texas A&M UP, 1993. 31.

Tillich, Paul. *Ultimate Concern: Tillich in Dialogue with D. Mackenzie Brown.* New York: Harper, 1967. Religion-Online Ed. Harry T. Adams and Grace C. Adams. 17 June 2005. www.religion-online.org/showchapter.asp?title=538&C=598.

Tucci, Guiseppe. *The Theory and Practice of the Mandala.* in Merton, *Asian Journal.* 81.

Turpin, Solveig, ed. *Rock Art and Cultural Processes.* Special Publication 3. San Antonio: Rock Art Foundation, 2002.

---."Seminole Sink: Excavations of a Vertical Shaft Tomb, Val Verde County." *Texas Plains Anthropologist,* Memoir 22, Vol. 33. November 1988.

---, ed. *Shamanism and Rock Art in North America.* Special Publication 1. San Antonio: Rock Art Foundation, 1994.

Vecsey, Christopher. *Imagine Ourselves Richly: Narratives of North American Indians.* New York: HarperCollins, 1991. 28, 29.

Zimmer, Heinrich. *The King and the Corpse.* Ed. Joseph Campbell. Bollingen Series XI. Princeton, NJ: Princeton UP, 1971. 3.

Zwinger, Ann Haymond. *The Mysterious Lands: A Naturalist Explores the Four Great Deserts of the Southwest.* New York: Truman, Talley, 1990. 8, 69.

Mary Locke Crosland Crofts lives in San Antonio and Langtry.